I0866458

CHAUMET IN MAJESTY

Jewels of Sovereigns Since 1780

CHAUMET IN MAJESTY

Jewels of Sovereigns Since 1780

GRIMALDI FORUM MONACO Flammarion

CONTENTS

PAGE 2 Joseph Chaumet (1852–1928), scrollwork tiara belonging to the Marquise de Talhouët (detail), 1908. Gold, silver, diamonds. Chaumet Collection, Paris, pages 128–29.
FACING PAGE Joseph Chaumet (1852–1928), wild rose tiara (detail), circa 1922. Platinum, diamonds, pearls. Private collection, page 226.

Palais de Monaco

July 2019

I am delighted to see the Grimaldi Forum sparkling this summer with Maison Chaumet's exhibition dedicated to the art of the tiara and, in particular, to sovereign jewels since the late eighteenth century.

This exceptional presentation showcases an array of superb jewelry parures loaned by great families, prestigious museums, and private collectors.

It illustrates the heightened elegance that the wearing of a tiara brings to a woman's aura and appearance.

This very special jewel, the reflection of an era, often draws its inspiration from nature.

This magnificent exhibition, enlightened by the expertise of its curators Stéphane Bern and Christophe Vachaudez, transports us in time and space, as we behold the supremely refined adornment of woman in all her splendor.

H.S.H. Prince Albert II of Monaco

Albert de Monaco

MAGNIFICENT ENCOUNTERS

There are moments in the history of a Maison that were simply meant to be. The exhibition *Chaumet in Majesty: Jewels of Sovereigns Since 1780* at the Grimaldi Forum in the Principality of Monaco is a truly brilliant example.

For more than two centuries, Chaumet has reinvented the art of jewelry, taking us on a journey far and wide, where the exceptional is the rule and beauty the goal. Here, time is of no importance. All that matters are the delight to the eye and the thrill of emotion.

And so for the paths of Chaumet and the Principality of Monaco to cross seemed the most natural thing in the world. On this precious jewel set upon the blue Mediterranean, living legends have thrived, created, and shone: crowned heads, not just of Europe, but of the entire world, figures of power, iconic artists, fashion arbiters, and society's movers and shakers all helped make Monaco a brilliant hub of excellence. Colette, Edith Wharton, F. Scott Fitzgerald, Louise de Vilmorin, Hector Berlioz, Gustave Eiffel, and Pablo Picasso all found creative opportunities in this gem of a setting, which offers up both the freedom of the open sea and the riches of the city.

They, among many other shining stars, chose the Principality and, driven by the same quest for perfection, chose Chaumet to turn their dreams into jewels.

And this is how, in a meeting of destinies, where the course of history fosters creative passion, Maison Chaumet and the Principality of Monaco have come together to share their fertile heritage, under the High Patronage of H.S.H. Prince Albert II.

JEAN-MARC MANSVELT
C.E.O. Chaumet

FACING PAGE *Firmament Apollinien* tiara, *La Nature de Chaumet* collection, 2016.

This catalog was published in conjunction with the exhibition *Chaumet in Majesty: Jewels of Sovereigns Since 1780* at the Grimaldi Forum Monaco from July 12 to August 28, 2019.

CURATORS

Stéphane Bern
Christophe Vachaudez

CHAUMET

Jean-Marc Mansvelt
C.E.O.

Claire Gannet
Heritage Director

Béatrice de Plinval
Honorary Curator of Heritage

GRIMALDI FORUM

Sylvie Biancheri
General Director

Catherine Alestchenkoff
Director of Cultural Events

Marie-Hélène Ballestri
Events Director

William Châtelain
Head of Studies and Design of Spaces

CATALOG AUTHORS (in order of appearance)

H.S.H. Prince Albert II of Monaco

Jean-Marc Mansvelt
C.E.O. Chaumet

Stéphane Bern
Guest curator of the exhibition

Christophe Vachaudez
Curator of the exhibition

Romain Condamine
Registrar of the Chaumet collections

Karine Huguenaud
Curator in charge of Chaumet exhibitions

FLAMMARION

EXECUTIVE EDITOR
Suzanne Tise-Isoré
Style & Design Collection

EDITORIAL COORDINATION
Lara Lo Calzo

EDITORIAL COORDINATION FOR CHAUMET
Karine Huguenaud

EDITORIAL ASSISTANT
Gwendoline Blanchard

GRAPHIC DESIGN
Bernard Lagacé and Lysandre Le Cléac'h

TRANSLATED FROM THE FRENCH BY
Alexandra Keens

COPY EDITING AND PROOFREADING
Lindsay Porter

PRODUCTION
Corinne Trovarelli

COLOR SEPARATION
Les Artisans du Regard, Paris

Printed in Italy by Musumeci

Simultaneously published in French as
Chaumet en Majesté. Joyaux de souveraines depuis 1780.

© Flammarion S.A., Paris, 2019
© Chaumet, 2019

English language edition
© Flammarion S.A., Paris, 2019
© Chaumet, 2019

All rights reserved for all countries. No part of this publication may be reproduced in any form or by any means, electronic, photocopy, information retrieval system, or otherwise, without written permission from Flammarion S.A.

Flammarion S.A.
87, quai Panhard-et-Levassor
75647 Paris cedex 13
editions.flammarion.com
styleetdesign-flammarion.com

19 20 21 3 2 1
ISBN: 978-2-08-020430-1
Legal Deposit: 07/2019

ACKNOWLEDGMENTS

Maison Chaumet and the exhibition curators wish to express their respectful gratitude to:

H.M. Queen Margrethe II of Denmark

HH.RR.HH the Grand Duke
and Grand Duchess of Luxembourg

H.S.H. Prince Albert II of Monaco

H.R.H. Princess of Hanover

Her Excellency Sheikha Al-Mayassa bint Hamad Al Thani

His Grace the Duke of Bedford

We extend our thanks to the public and private institutions whose generous cooperation enabled this exhibition to take place.

BELGIUM

Antwerp, DIVA museum – Wim Nys, Ann Verbecque, Romy Cockx
Kortrijk, Epoque Fine Jewels – Nicole Verschuere, Patricia de Wit, Bart Peers

CZECH REPUBLIC

Prague, Museum of Decorative Arts – PhDr. Helena Koenigsmarková, Ivana Quilezová, Petra Matějovičová

FRANCE

Auxerre, Salle d'Eckmühl, Blocqueville collection – Delphine Lannaud, Stéphanie Guyot-Nourry
Compiègne, Musées et Domaines Nationaux de Compiègne – Rodolphe Rapetti, Laure Chabanne, Gilles Legrand
Paris, Fondation Dosne-Thiers, Institut de France – François d'Orcival, Sandrine Folpini, Agnès Champagnac
Paris, Fondation Napoléon – Victor-André Masséna Prince of Essling, Duc de Rivoli, Pierre Branda, Élodie Lefort, Céline Clouet
Paris, Musée du Louvre, Department of Decorative Arts – Jean-Luc Martinez, Jannic Durand
Paris, Musée de la Vie Romantique – Jérôme Farigoule, Gaëlle Rio
Paris, BNP Paribas – Pierre de Pellegars, Christiane de Fleurieu, Nathalie Sauvanet
Nice, Musée Masséna – Jean-Pierre Barbero
Rueil-Malmaison, Musée National des Châteaux de Malmaison et de Bois-Préau – Amaury Lefébure, Céline Meunier, Élodie Vaysse, Stéphane Macrez
Sèvres, Cité de la Céramique – Romane Sarfati
Versailles, Musée national des Châteaux de Versailles et de Trianon – Catherine Pégard, Laurent Salomé, Frédéric Lacaille

JAPAN

Tokyo, Albion Art Collection – Kazumi Arikawa, Keiko Horii

LUXEMBOURG

Grand-Ducal Collection – Déborah Schott

MONACO

The Prince's Palace Collections – Hervé Irien, Christian Selvatico

NETHERLANDS

The Hague, Royal Collections – Dr Flip Maarschalkerweerd, Claudia Marteense-van Ham, Claudia Hörster, Lisa van der Borch, Sander Wolterink

PORTUGAL

Lisbon, Palácio Nacional da Ajuda – José Alberto Ribeiro, Teresa Maranhas

QATAR

Qatar Museums – Ahmad Al Namla, Clémence Marie Bergal, Hicham Al Baker

SWITZERLAND

Geneva, Faerber Collection – Thomas and Katharina Faerber, Ayena de Bourgues

UNITED KINGDOM

The Woburn Abbey Collection of His Grace the Duke of Bedford – Matthew Hirst

We are deeply grateful for the support of all the collection managers and collectors who wish to remain anonymous.

H.S.H. Prince Charles-Henri de Lobkowicz

H.S.H. Prince Olivier de Croÿ-Roeulx

Stephen De Bono, Brian De Bono, Elena Datrino, Marco Datrino, Alejandro Espejo Fernandez, Louise Hung, Muguette Jumeau, Charles-Henri Keller, Sabrina Koesharto at Christie's, The Lin Family, Nicholas Norton, Jonathan Norton, Francis Norton, Murielle Prieur, Benoît Repellin at Sotheby's, Diana Scarisbrick, Hisako Yoshikawa, Patrizia Webb, Wilfried Zeisler.

THE SYMBOLISM OF TIARAS

STÉPHANE BERN

WEALTH, POWER, STRENGTH, AND VICTORY; WISDOM AND SACREDNESS; CROWNING SYMBOL OF LOVE: EVER SINCE CLASSICAL ANTIQUITY, TIARAS HAVE BEEN AN OBJECT OF FASCINATION FOR THEIR SYMBOLIC DIMENSION, AS WELL AS FOR THEIR ARTISTRY IN DISPLAYING A PROFUSION OF DIAMONDS AND GEMSTONES IN THE PREVAILING FASHION OF THE DAY.

During the Belle Époque, Marcel Proust, in his *In Search of Lost Time*, viewed a tiara as the ultimate key to high society, describing the Duchess of Guermantes as "looking splendid in her emerald tiara and a pink dress with a long train." A tiara truly incarnates transfiguration and majesty, a fairytale transformation: upon donning a tiara, a woman enters a magical world. The perfect family heirloom, steeped in tradition and history, a tiara projects a halo of light that glorifies the entire lineage, attaining everything eternal and spiritual. Countless brides have perpetuated the long, historic tradition of bridal crowns—whether a wreath of flowers or a family tiara—which indicates both the loss of innocence and a consecration of love. The most emblematic of these gems is certainly the Queen of Sweden's famous tiara of pearls and cameos, originally made for Empress Joséphine shortly before her divorce from Napoleon in 1809, by Marie-Étienne Nitot, founder of the Maison Chaumet. The cameos depict the story of Cupid and Psyche. This legendary tiara has survived the ages, handed down from generation to generation. It looks similar to the one in Ferdinand-Louis Quaglia's miniature portrait of Empress Joséphine, done in 1814, the year of her death. Historians are not entirely certain what happened to the tiara after Joséphine died, but it was apparently inherited by her son Eugène, Duke of Leuchtenberg. In 1823, his daughter, Josephine of Leuchtenberg, married the Swedish crown prince Oscar—later King Oscar I—and the cameo tiara thereby entered the royal Swedish collection. As queen, Joséphine wore it on several occasions when posing for official portraits. Upon her death it went to her sole daughter, Eugénie, who died without issue and left it to her nephew, Prince Eugen, who also remained unmarried and thus lent the tiara to his niece, Princess Margaret of Connaught, the crown princess of Sweden, who was said to have worn it once to her children's nursery in order to recount its history, telling the children how the tiara once belonged to their famous ancestor, Empress Joséphine of France. In 1932 Prince Eugen of Sweden gave it as a wedding gift to his grand-niece, Sybilla of Saxe-Coburg and Gotha upon her marriage to Prince Gustaf Adolf. Sybilla would bequeath the cameo tiara to her only son, today's King Carl XVI Gustaf, as a personal possession: he lent it to his sisters, Birgitta and Désirée, who wore it on their respective wedding days. It also crowned the head of his fiancée, Silvia, upon their own marriage on June 19, 1976. Crown Princess Victoria of Sweden then wore it in turn upon her marriage, to Daniel Westling, on June 19, 2010, exactly thirty-fours years after her mother. The cameo tiara still graces Queen Silvia during Swedish court festivities—official dinners, state visits, Nobel Prize award ceremonies, and so on—and testifies to a historical continuity that underscores both the royal function and that function's deep roots in the past.

FACING PAGE Fredrik Westin (1782–1862), *Joséphine of Sweden* wearing the pearl tiara and necklace inherited from Empress Joséphine, 1837. Oil on canvas. Rosendal Palace, Stockholm, Maltesholm Castle, Kristianstad.

The historic career of this glamorous tiara, made by imperial court jeweler Nitot, would be merely anecdotal if it didn't also incarnate the role of tiara as symbol. The tiara has become a kind of "civilian" version of a crown. Like a crown, a tiara is associated with the qualities of elevation, superiority, and sacredness—a gift from above. In Ancient Greece and Rome, it symbolized dedication to the gods, whose statues were wreathed with leaves of the trees and fruit associated with them. In his *Theogony*, the Greek poet Hesiod described Pandora, the first woman created by Zeus, as bedecked by Athena and Hephaestus with "a golden band on her head…on it [were] fashioned many skillful things, a wonder to behold." Etymologically, the Greek, and later Roman, term *diadem* means "band" ("to bind from both sides"), sometimes used synonymously with that other Greek word, "tiara". Monuments, sculptures, and coins display numerous examples of these graceful headbands made with natural materials: flowers, ears of wheat, acanthus or olive leaves, shells or feathers. From this time onward, wreaths of foliage of sacred trees became a symbol of glory. They graced the brows of priests and soothsayers, while winners of the Olympic games received a wreath as the prize of victory. In classical antiquity, victors were crowned with wreaths of laurel—the Latin term *laureatus*, "crowned with laurel," is the root of the term "laureate" for the holder of an outstanding award or achievement—while brides wore tiaras of myrtle, symbol of love and marriage. These trophies became permanent and everlasting once they were worked in gold, both malleable and precious. Such adornment swiftly became the prerogative of victorious generals, famous poets, triumphant athletes, inspired musicians, and distinguished scholars. It was only later, under Alexander the Great, that this headdress became the symbol of royalty, probably inspired by his conquest, in 333 BCE, of Persia, where kings wore similar headdresses. The Greek word "tiara", in fact, was originally Persian, and indicated high rank. Its symbolism was related to its lofty position on the head, simultaneously displaying elevation, power, and recognition. Whereas Greek and Etruscan tiaras reproduced nature's abundance in simple gold, those made during the Roman Empire, while less fine and delicate, added riches in the form of amethysts, pearls, emeralds, sapphires, and even diamonds. In Rome, a narrow bandeau or tiara, worn on the forehead, symbolized absolute power, becoming indissociable with the image of emperor and empress.

THE DIADEM, OR ORNAMENTAL HEADBAND, WAS AN EMBLEM OF ELEVATION, SUPERIORITY, AND SACREDNESS, A GIFT FROM ABOVE. IN ANCIENT GREECE AND ROME, IT SYMBOLIZED THE CONSECRATION OF THE GODS; THEIR STATUES WERE CROWNED WITH THE LEAVES OF THE TREES AND FRUITS THAT WERE DEDICATED TO THEM. IN THE GREEK POET HESIOD'S *THEOGONY*, HEPHAESTUS AND ATHENA PLACE ON THE HEAD OF PANDORA, THE FIRST WOMAN CREATED BY ZEUS, "A GOLDEN BAND," DECORATED WITH "MANY SKILLFUL THINGS, A WONDER TO BEHOLD."

With the arrival of Christianity and the fall of the eastern Roman Empire, tiaras tended to vanish. It was henceforth

FACING PAGE Alexandre Cabanel (1823–1889), *Pandora* (detail), 1873. Oil on canvas. The Walters Art Museum, Baltimore, MD.

the glory of God that counted—mortals had to display more humility. Tiaras made a return to fashion in the last quarter of the eighteenth century, when Europe rediscovered the ancient world. But by the end of that century, diadems were no longer the sole prerogative of royalty, and tiaras were being worn by brides of varying rank and social status. A tiara became a crowning symbol of love. That is how, in an artistic saga forged by Nitot, Fossin, Morel, and Chaumet in the nineteenth and twentieth centuries, tiaras regained their full role, featuring emblematic jewels that put the seal on marriages among major aristocratic families and industrial dynasties, such as the tiara made in 1919 for the wedding of Hedwige de La Rochefoucauld (daughter of the Duke of Doudeauville) to Prince Sixtus of Bourbon-Parma. Even in today's high-society weddings, the bride's veil will inevitably be held in place by a family heirloom, a tiara passed down from generation to generation. Formerly, in France, the groom would bestow upon the bride a rich set of gifts that included family jewels, to which he might add a specially made new piece. Similarly, throughout the nineteenth century—and even the early twentieth—tiaras continued to symbolize fame and success, notably crowning the ravishing heads of actresses and dancers—the "queens of Paris"—not only on stage by also in town, as the proud sign of a generous husband or lover such as Sacha Guitry or Count Henckel von Donnersmarck.

Tiara designs often recall the ancient motifs of flowers and other highly symbolic plant life: ears of wheat for fertility, laurel and acanthus leaves for success and fame, and even the famous love knot, also known as a Hercules knot, symbolizing strength and protection, because the ancient Greek hero used that knot to tie the paws of the Nemean lion he slew. It is entertaining to note that William Moulton Marston set a tiara on the forehead of his super hero, Wonder Woman, as though marking both her Amazonian heritage—Princess Diana of Themyscira—and her magical, supernatural powers.

FACING PAGE Walker & Boutall, *The Duchess of Portland as Duchess of Savoy, at the Devonshire House Ball*, 1897. National Portrait Gallery, London.
BELOW Georges Rouget (1783–1869), *The Religious Marriage of Napoleon I and Marie-Louise in the Salon Carré at the Louvre, on April 2, 1810 (detail)*, 1810. Oil on canvas. Musée National des Châteaux de Versailles et de Trianon, Versailles.

As the apotheosis of jewelry and a symbol of the Maison Chaumet, tiaras became open to all influences and all styles. An emblem of power as much as a fashion accessory, they ranged from the extremely classic to the highly extravagant, crowning ceremonial and social events in every day and age. The rise of Marie-Étienne Nitot, Paris jeweler established in 1780, cannot be attributed solely to the family legend—an unattested anecdote—of Nitot's act of bravery in halting the runaway horse pulling the dangerously careening carriage of First Consul Bonaparte. Soon to be crowned Emperor Napoleon, the new Augustus—in every sense of the term—realized that if he wanted to reign over France he would have to sparkle. The neoclassical style was still in full swing thanks to the recent rediscovery of antiquity, and thus the Maison Chaumet—via jeweler Nitot—began to write itself into French history by setting the regalia of imperial government with wonderful gemstones. Ancient patterns and shapes came back to life: ears of wheat, acanthus and laurel leaves, palmettes, scrollwork, Greek-key patterns, carnations and pansies, as well as the cameos and intaglios that Empress Joséphine so loved. Napoleon wanted Nitot to adorn all the ladies of his court so that their unprecedented glitter would light up the world. Nitot obliged, making jewelry for Caroline Bonaparte (Queen of Naples), Élisa Bonaparte (Grand Duchess of Tuscany), Pauline Bonaparte, Hortense de Beauharnais (Napoleon's stepdaughter, Queen of Holland), and Stéphanie de Beauharnais (his adopted daughter, Grand Duchess of Baden). To please his second wife, Empress Marie-Louise, Napoleon ordered a stunning set of wedding gifts that notably included a parure and tiara set with the nineteenth century's most fabulous diamonds. The tiara, with its expressive artistry directly inspired by antiquity, became emblematic of Empire-style jewelry. Like a crown, the diamond-studded tiara was a symbol of power, affirming social preeminence through superlative sparkle that inspired reverence and respect.

As newly independent states emerged, all of Europe began acquiring such items, and the new sovereigns placed orders with Nitot, Fossin, Morel, and Chaumet. The Duchy of Bavaria, elevated to a kingdom by Napoleon, acquired tiaras that can still be seen in the Schatzkammer in Munich. The Maison Chaumet made no fewer than three thousand five hundred tiaras in two centuries of uncontested reign. Beginning with Napoleon, all ladies invited to a ball would don their finest attire and jewels, the glittering symbols of their wealth and social status. From London to Naples, from Lisbon to Copenhagen, from Saint Petersburg to Madrid, and from Bucharest to Berlin, no woman would think of attending a society dinner without a tiara on her head. Throughout her long life, Queen Elizabeth II has refrained from ever appearing bare-headed: in daytime she wears a hat, in the evening a tiara. This ancient tradition is respected by high society even today, while during the nineteenth century dynasties of industrialists adopted this symbol when marrying their offspring to grand aristocratic families. Meanwhile, buccaneering American heiresses—Gould, Vanderbilt, Bell, Belmont—would go to the altar in France or Britain wearing a tiara as freshly made as their fathers' fortunes. In London, that realm of unbroken tradition, no noblewoman would be without her own, from the Duchess of Marlborough to the Duchess of Manchester via the Duchesses of Roxburghe, Devonshire, and Westminster, not forgetting Lady Churchill. That tradition survives today during state dinners at Buckingham Palace and marriages among the landed gentry. The debutants' ball in Paris has adopted this aristocratic practice, bringing tiaras back into fashion. Indeed, these head ornaments still spark dreams, still signify high society and the achievement of grand social status; as in ancient Greece, they still convey power and glory, honor and success, valor and merit. Reinterpreted and refined for the past two hundred years by the Maison Chaumet, tiaras of diamonds and other gemstones have remained faithful to their primal symbolic function as a ritual wreath of leaves and flowers that celebrates the cult of nature even as it crowns the heads of victorious, accomplished, or highly honored individuals.

FACING PAGE Henry Clarke (1918–1996), *Anne Gunning Parker*, future Lady Nutting, wearing a Chaumet tiara that converts into a necklace, 1953.

PAGES 20–21 Attributed to Nitot & Fils, cameo tiara belonging to Empress Joséphine, circa 1810. Gold, agate cameos, natural pearls. Slottsmuseum, Kungl. Husgerådskammaren, Collection of the Swedish Royal Family, Stockholm.

SACRE
DE
SA MAJESTÉ
L'EMPEREUR
NAPOLÉON Ier

MAJESTIC CHAUMET

CHRISTOPHE VACHAUDEZ

FOR OVER TWO CENTURIES, THE MAISON CHAUMET'S WORKSHOPS HAVE BEEN NOTEWORTHY FOR THEIR IMAGINATION AND INVENTIVENESS, MAKING TIARAS AND EXTRAORDINARY PARURES FOR A SOPHISTICATED CLIENTELE ATTRACTED TO THEIR QUALITY AND ORIGINALITY AND THEIR PEERLESS DESIGNS.

Throughout its long history, from the time of Marie-Étienne Nitot to the present, company registers and visitors' books testify to the trust and loyalty displayed by its high-ranking clientele, ranging from Emperor Napoleon to the Maharaja of Indore, from Empress Eugénie to Grand Duchess Maria Pavlovna, and from the Yusupov princes to Victoria Eugenie, Queen of Spain. Aristocrats and members of European courts, Indian princes, those in the world of art and letters, collectors, leading financiers, and rich industrialists have all placed their faith in this great French jeweler, intrinsically associated with head ornaments such as crowns, tiaras, bandeaux, and aigrettes.

This affinity is wonderfully illustrated by the replicas of such pieces called "maillechorts"—made of nickel silver—which still grace the walls of a room in the former Baudard de Sainte-James residence, now the Chaumet showroom on Place Vendôme in Paris. Never had a jeweler designed so many tiaras, and the tradition not only carries on today but also looks resolutely toward the future. The carefully conserved collection of heritage items recounts this history in detail, thanks to drawings, albums, written archives, and photographic records, constituting a kind of detailed register. Studying this material takes us back to the roots of the noble jewelry firm, the better to grasp the creative essence that infuses *Chaumet in Majesty*.

FACING PAGE Andrea Appiani the Elder (1754–1817), *Portrait of Empress Joséphine as Queen of Italy* (detail). Oil on canvas. Châteaux de Malmaison et Bois-Préau, Rueil-Malmaison.

It is tempting to begin with "Once upon a time," so unique was the story of Marie-Etienne Nitot. The son of a "wholesale fish merchant" who provisioned Paris,[1] he strove for a career as a goldsmith. He eventually worked with the jeweler to the king, Ange-Joseph Aubert, as confirmed by the latter's ledgers. Aubert was keeper of the royal gems under Louis XV and Louis XVI, and supplied the likes of Queen Marie-Antoinette and the king's sister, Madame Élisabeth.[2] In 1790 Nitot was asked to verify the inventory of the Crown's gemstones and jewelry. His advice was sought again when, during the Consulate period (1799–1804), a selection of the finest stones in the government's Cabinet de Minéralogie had to be made. That was also when Nitot was commissioned to make the sword for First Consul Napoleon Bonaparte, and then—during the First Empire (1805–15)—a tiara presented to Pope Pius VII. Once completed, the precious tiara was given to François-Renault, Nitot's son, to take it to Rome. Along the way, he stopped in Milan, where Napoleon and Joséphine were staying, to show them the tiara. Having taken several parures with him, he seized the opportunity to show them to Empress Joséphine, who was so charmed that she soon had the Nitots join the select group of official suppliers to the imperial court. Delighted to be named "Jewelers in Ordinary to the Empress" in 1805, Nitot & Fils placed the imperial coat of arms on the front of their new Paris premises. That was the start of their meteoric rise.

Napoleon, aware of the fragility of his new rank of emperor, wanted at all cost to consolidate the image of himself and his court, thereby legitimizing the power invested in him at his coronation. He thus instituted a policy of ostentation that would spur the rise and expansion of luxury goods. Jewelry obviously held pride of place, adding unprecedented splendor to festivities modeled on those of the ancien régime. Napoleon himself insisted that life at court be conducted like a perfectly choreographed ballet, everyone respecting to the letter the dress codes required for each occasion. Finery was considerably heightened through the addition of a belt or a hair comb, and tiaras made a notable comeback, worn either crown-like on the top of the head or else clasped to the forehead, above the eyebrows, in bandeau-style. Classical antiquity, the stylistic model favored by Napoleon, also inspired fashion designers and jewelers, who often worked together on female attire. In fact, flowing gowns with high waists, often underscored by a belt, featured low, broad necklines with fancy trim that left ample room on the neck and breast for the large necklaces typical of the full, opulent style developed by Nitot. That style was marked by clear, symmetrical designs with large-sized stones that made an even greater impression, and it developed a decorative idiom based on Greek and Roman architecture, employing palmettes, scrollwork, and Greek-key patterns, as well as acanthus, olive boughs, and laurel leaves—and, of course, ears of wheat, that attribute of Ceres, goddess of fertility. The gold laurel leaves crowning Napoleon's head were matched by the diamond-studded laurel leaves on a tiara worn by Joséphine at the coronation. Elaborate hairstyles dubbed "Titus," "Ninon," and "Ceres" often called for a bejeweled wheat-ear that went well with curls and real flowers. The highly popular wheat-ears were among Joséphine's favorite ornaments, and she wore them for her first official act as empress when awarding crosses of the Legion of Honor on July 14, 1804. And when she found herself in Bordeaux in 1808, she wrote to her daughter asking to borrow a few pieces; her letter of April 17 reads, "You know, dear Hortense, that the only diamonds I have are a very fine necklace. If you can do without your ears of wheat and two strings of stones, I would be grateful if you could send them to me here."[3] When Hortense led a quadrille at a ball given at the Tuileries Palace on April 20, 1806, "all the ladies wore diamond-studded ears of wheat."[4] Nitot apparently appreciated this design, for he had an ear of wheat etched on his hallmark, and he made dozens for the wedding trousseaus he was commissioned to supply. When Joséphine's niece, Stéphanie de Beauharnais, married Grand Duke Charles of Baden, they sparkled on her. "The emperor, in Spanish dress, gave the hand of the bride who wore a silver-studded white gown, adorned from top to bottom with diamond ears of wheat and bouquets of orange flowers, whose train of silver gauze seemed straight out of a fairy tale."[5] Meanwhile, the grand, elaborate diamond parure delivered in 1811 for Napoleon's marriage to Archduchess Marie-Louise included no fewer than one hundred and fifty gold-backed ears of wheat that could be mixed and matched. Finally, an inventory drawn up in 1804 indicates that Joséphine already owned forty-three, matched to Greek-key plaques of brilliants and a bandeau tiara of six cameos.[6]

Key patterns and cameos were combined to celebrate classical antiquity once again. In January 1808, Nitot showed the imperial couple a complete parure featuring forty-five cameos and thirty-six intaglios from the Cabinet des Médailles. The art of stone carving enjoyed its moment of glory as daytime parures, which usually included a tiara, soon featured malachite, coral, sardius, and onyx, or even tiny mosaics and fine hardstones. Nor were gemstones overlooked, for Nitot redesigned a ruby necklace for Joséphine in 1808.

ELABORATE HAIRSTYLES DUBBED "TITUS," "NINON," AND "CERES" OFTEN CALLED FOR A BEJEWELED WHEAT-EAR THAT WENT WELL WITH CURLS AND REAL FLOWERS. THE HIGHLY POPULAR WHEAT-EARS WERE AMONG JOSÉPHINE'S FAVORITE ORNAMENTS.

FACING PAGE Jean-Baptiste-Jacques Augustin (1759–1832), *Portrait of Empress Joséphine* (detail) wearing a wheat-ear tiara, early nineteenth century. Gouache, watercolor. Fondation Napoléon, Paris.

Every wedding meant more business for the jeweler, who supplied a diamond parure valued at 300,000 francs when Catharina of Württemberg married Jérôme Bonaparte. Her tiara of palmettes and fleurons wonderfully illustrated the Empire style ennobled by Nitot and exported to foreign courts thanks to the imperial practice of diplomatic and family gifts. This system of imperial presents regularly displayed a generosity designed to enhance the regime's reputation and flaunt its prosperity and included monogrammed snuffboxes, watches, pendants, and fancy jewelry. François-Regnault Nitot[7] was awarded the most extravagant orders when Napoleon married Archduchess Marie-Louise of Austria in 1810. Napoleon wanted to dazzle this niece of Marie-Antoinette, and showered her in jewels. The first parures she was given were diamonds heightened with historic crown jewels ("in the ornaments of which were found the palmettes and husks typical of the style of that time")[8], followed by parures of emeralds and diamonds, of pearls, and of opals and diamonds. Over the months her collection of jewelry grew to include oriental rubies, amethysts, turquoises, sapphires, and pink topazes—not to mention day wear.

When the imperial couple's son, styled the Roi de Rome, was born in 1811, Napoleon's munificence increased, and Nitot notably supplied two parures of Brazilian rubies and brilliants, two parures of emeralds and brilliants, and four other parures set with balas rubies, amethysts, opals, and chrysoprases, and a necklace of bezel-set stones and twelve ears of wheat. The dignitaries who officiated at the new child's baptism in Nôtre-Dame Cathedral were presented with jewels. The new empress, who fulfilled her husband's wishes by always appearing in glittering jewelry, was given a splendid diamond necklace with briolette-cut diamonds and pendants. Even if the grand style slowly gave way to Romantic "jewels of sentiment," orders continued to flow in to the jewelers. On January 21, 1812, Nitot & Fils delivered to the empress a bracelet of braided hair with a lock of the Roi de Rome's hair set beneath a large flat diamond, flanked by colored stones spelling out the name Napoleon.[9] Joséphine, too, owned acrostic bracelets similar to the one that Napoleon gave his sister Elisa when her daughter was born, and to the ones given to Marie-Louise in 1810.

When the Empire fell in 1815, François-Regnault Nitot handed the reins to his head of workshop, Jean-Baptiste

FACING PAGE Jean-Baptiste Paulin Guérin (1783–1855) after François Gérard (1770–1837), *Marie-Louise, Empress of the French*, wearing the topaz and diamond parure by Nitot (detail). Oil on canvas, Châteaux de Versailles et de Trianon, Versailles.
BELOW Innocent-Louis Goubaud (1780–1847), *Baptism of the Roi de Rome at Notre-Dame de Paris, on June 10, 1811* (detail), 1813. Black chalk. Châteaux de Versailles et de Trianon, Versailles.

"WE NOTICED A WHOLE CROP OF RED CURRANTS IN THE BLONDE HAIR OF A BEAUTIFUL FOREIGNER: EACH OF THE CURRANTS AMIDST THE GREEN LEAVES WAS SET WITH A LARGE RUBY."

Fossin, who in 1830 was joined by his own son, Jules. An interest in alternative styles—plainer, or based on other influences—had already emerged, as heralded by the Gothic-style belt worn by Empress Marie-Louise, and by the hydrangea-themed garlands that she owned personally. Although the restored Bourbon monarchs sought to revive the grandiose style of earlier centuries, society aspired to something lighter, and soon adopted the naturalistic style promoted by Fossin, even if he continued to produce items featuring palmettes, acanthus leaves, and Greek-key patterns. The Duchess of Berry, who liked novelty, honored the jeweler in 1824 with a warrant of official supplier to the royal children of France. In 1819, a bouquet of brilliants that Fossin displayed at a national exposition sparked admiration, and Henri Vever concluded that "it is as a jeweler that Fossin merits special mention... above all because he was the first... of his day who tried to get closer to nature in his pretty designs of bouquets, which he then executed in brilliants."[10] Thus highly fashionable morning glory, vine leaves, and, above all, reeds began to join olive branches, chestnut leaves, mangrove trees, and hawthorn around necks and in hair. These veritable articulated branches and foliate tiaras were enlivened with bunches of grapes or clusters of raspberries or strawberries. They evolved into airy aigrettes and teeming bouquets, blooming with eglantine, jasmine, camellia, campanula, daisies, hollyhock, heliotrope, fuchsia, and rosebuds, often set *"en trembleuse."* A newspaper of the day described a society ball where Fossin's loyal clients mingled, such as "Madame Baring, crowned in pansies and amethysts, the Duchess of Istria, with tufts of Parma violet and red carnations, the Duchess of Montebello adorned in white roses, and the Duchess of Elchingen wearing a pink geranium tiara."[11] *Les Modes* even wrote, "We noticed a whole crop of red currants in the blonde hair of a beautiful foreigner: each of the currants amidst the green leaves was set with a large ruby."[12] These head ornaments were often transformable into other pieces, and thus could also be worn as brooches, for example.

Fossin, joined by his son Jules—awarded the title of Jeweler to the King in 1832 by Louis-Philippe—made the bride's wedding gifts for the marriage of the Duke of Orléans in 1837, and boasted a clientele of bankers, aristocrats, and courtiers. His reputation in France and abroad has been confirmed by an unpublished document from the grand-ducal archives in Wiesbaden. The Duke of Nassau wished to modernize his jewelry, and to that end sent his jeweler, Jacob Speltz, to Paris to study the latest fashions. Speltz reported on his mission, writing in a letter dated February 2, 1829: "As soon as I arrived in Paris my first task was to seek out the man whose taste and skill have made him the marvel of his day—Monsieur Nitot (jeweler to Napoleon's court). I was so pleased to make his acquaintance, and after frequent exchanges of our wine, he told me that while garlands were suitable for balls, a full-dress tiara, indispensible for a princely state, must be entirely arabesque."[13]

Fossin, who also supplied the regalia for King Otto of Greece in 1832, pursued his stylistic explorations. Employing an idealized aesthetic, he promoted the Gothic and Renaissance revival styles, designing tiara-coronets with heraldic fleurons for the Duchess of Palmela and a Hohenzollern princess. Set in a Francis I style, diamonds glittered all the more in the hair, when not dangling from the temples, falling in cascades like the side curls of Marie Mancini, Cardinal Mazarin's niece. In 1840, Count Anatoly Demidov chose Fossin to make the jewelry for his future wife, Princess Mathilde Bonaparte. The workshop created five full parures, the first of emeralds, the second of sapphires, the third of topazes, the fourth of turquoises, and the fifth of opals, all set off with brilliants. The fleuron tiaras came with matching garlands, bracelets, earrings, necklaces, and bowknot brooches (known as *sévignés*).

FACING PAGE Attributed to Jules Fossin (1808–1869), redcurrant leaves hair ornaments, 1853.
Gold, silver, diamonds. Private collection.

The Revolution of 1848 produced no major changes for the jeweler, who, of course, lost his royal patrons, yet remained loyal to the house of Orléans. This cooled his relationship to Empress Eugénie, who had been a long-time Fossin client. The names of august families like the Harcourts and La Rouchefoucaulds were joined on the client books by those associated with the new empire, such as Mouchy, Cambacérès, and Bassano, not to mention ever greater numbers of bankers and industrialists who henceforth coexisted with foreign princes in the growing sales ledgers. The jewelry firm, which glittered at the International Expositions of 1851, 1855, 1862, and 1867, opened a branch in London and, thanks to the intercession of the Belgian queen, Louise of Orléans, the director of the branch—Jean-Valentin Morel, the former head of Fossin's Paris workshop—received a warrant as official supplier to Queen Victoria. Morel was assisted by his son Prosper, who then took over from Jules Fossin in Paris in 1862. Empress Eugénie's admiration for Marie-Antoinette led to a return of bows, ribbons, fretwork, and key patterns, borrowed from the decorative idiom of the Louis-XVI period. Pearls retained resounding appeal, and were often more prized than diamonds as naturalism remained as popular as ever. The fall of the Second Empire brought an instability that further increased the urge to express royalist loyalties by wearing a tiara, or to assert one's status through lavish finery. In 1885, Joseph Chaumet, who had long worked in the company workshop, married Prosper Morel's daughter, Marie. He succeeded his father-in-law as head of the firm in 1889. Two years later, Chaumet oversaw one of the most important sets of wedding gifts in the company's history, namely the one offered to Dona Carlotta-Maximiliana Escandón when she married Don Felipe Falcó, 8th Duke of Montellano. The tiara in the matching set featured bowknots set with turquoises. During this same period, Chaumet delivered a clover tiara to the Duke of Luynes (1889) and another with reed decoration to the Duchess of Harcourt (1892), while fleurs-de-lis featured on the coronet made for Archduchess Maria Dorothea of Austria, who in 1896 married the Duke of Orléans, a pretender to the French throne. Set entirely in diamonds, the coronet was financed by a subscription organized by royalist ladies. As the peerless master jeweler of the Belle Époque, Joseph Chaumet was not seduced by the siren song of art nouveau as exemplified by René Lalique, yet his extremely delicate designs were infused with nature in all its splendor. Poet Paul Claudel might have penned some of the lines of *La Mystique des Pierres Précieuses* (The Mystique of Gemstones) while contemplating Chaumet's magic:

"These insects, all gleaming, golden jewels; the drop of dew that glitters on the tip of its blade of grass on a May morning; the black-iced tree, a warrior from head to toe in its suit of glass and its harness of fire, chiming with winter's sunbeam; and, finally, the little star, tiny as a pinprick, first discerned, then followed by the bigger one, like a drop of elixir rejoicing on dawn's bandeau."[14]

BELOW Joseph Chaumet (1852–1928), drawing studio, sketch for the lily flower tiara belonging to Princess Stéphanie of Belgium, 1907. Graphite pencil. Chaumet Collection, Paris.
FACING PAGE Princess Stéphanie of Belgium, wife of Archduke Rudolf of Austria, wearing the lily flower tiara made by Chaumet, 1908.

During this period, aigrettes offered a delightful alternative to the more imposing tiaras—a trembling feather might spring from a hummingbird, a crescent moon, a star, or a sun. Wing-themed aigrettes, often transformable into brooches, turned elegant ladies into messengers of the gods. In 1906 Empress Eugénie selected a diamond aigrette for her goddaughter, Princess Victoria Eugenie, who that year married King Alfonso XIII of Spain. The Princess of Ligne preferred openwork designs set with rubies, whereas Gertrude Payne Whitney fell for a pair of wings set with translucent blue enamel, having already acquired a sun studded with rubies.

Chaumet won gold medals at International Expositions in Paris (1900), Saint Louis (1904), Liège (1905), and Milan (1906), and in 1905 opened a London branch that soon drew the Duke of Westminster as well as the Duchesses of Manchester, Roxburghe, and Marlborough. Early in the century, Princess Henckel von Donnersmarck consigned her pear-shaped emeralds to Chaumet in order to have them set on a tiara, while in 1899 Grand Duchess Maria Pavlovna (the aunt of Czar Nicholas II) bought a bold "waterfall" tiara, emblematic of a house style that drew inspiration, like no other jeweler, from water in all its forms—cascading, frost-nipped, frozen, or solidified. Meanwhile, the use of platinum made for settings that were stronger, yet lighter and airier, as seen in a carnation tiara ordered by Madame de Wendel in 1905.

Chaumet's prestige increased still further in 1907 when it moved to Place Vendôme. On one hand, the Maison continued to produce designs from its traditional repertoire, while on the other it innovated by adopting the purer, streamlined look of the "modern" style. Thus the Marquise de Talhouët's scrollwork tiara (1908), Countess Geneviève de Chaponay's bowknot and drapery tiara (1910), and Princess Stephanie of Belgium's fleur-de-lis and interlaced-reed tiara (1907) could coexist with Countess Nostitz's geometric tiara (1909), the Duchess of Medinaceli's radial shield tiara (1912), and Princess Irina Yusupov's supple, sun-themed tiara (1914).

FACING PAGE Madame Yevonde (1893–1975), *Louis Mountbatten, 1st Earl Mountbatten of Burma, and Edwina, Countess Mountbatten of Burma*, 1937. Vivex colour print
BELOW Sapphire and diamond parure made for the wedding basket of gifts for Princess Alice of Bourbon-Parma, 1936. Print from gelatin silver-bromide glass negative. Chaumet Archives, Paris.

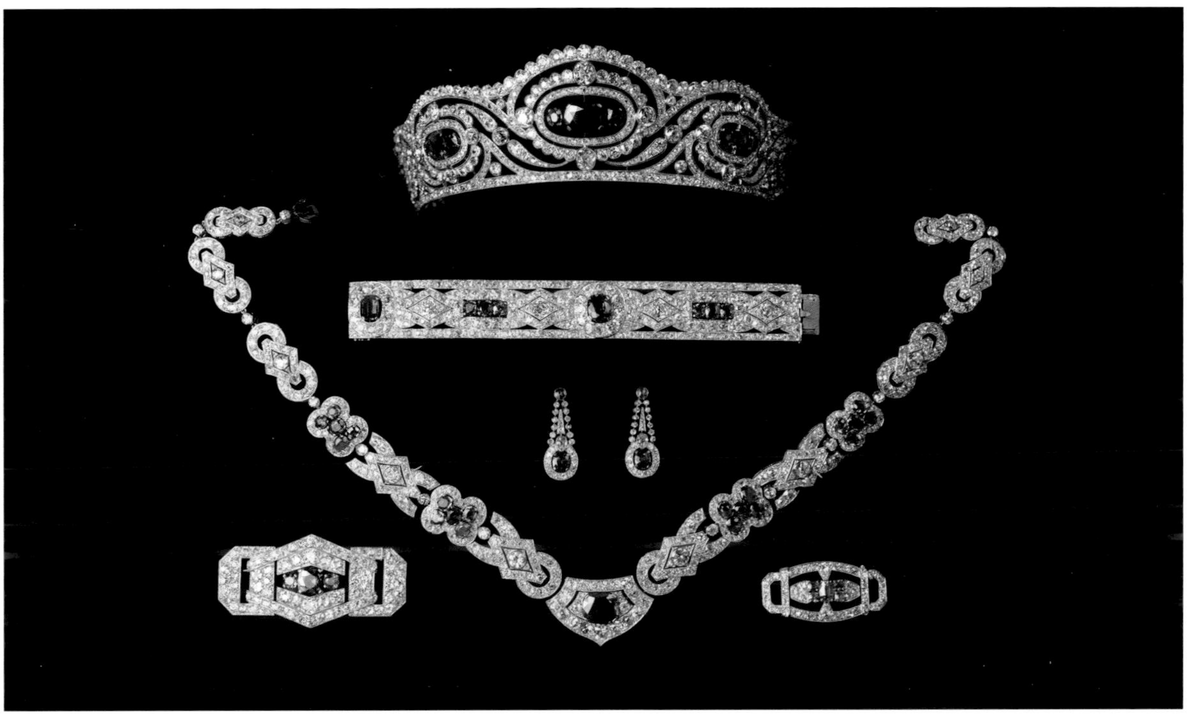

World War I put a temporary brake on the new movement, which finally triumphed at the International Exhibition of Modern Decorative and Industrial Arts in Paris in 1925.

In 1919, Chaumet was directly involved in the first major postwar society event, the marriage of Hedwige de La Rochefoucauld to Prince Sixtus of Bourbon-Parma. Charged with producing the bride's wedding gifts, Chaumet designed a tiara of stylized fuchsias that perfectly conveyed a stylistic evolution toward more radical geometry. In 1926, a tiara acquired by Grand Duchess Charlotte of Luxembourg was an unimpeachable example of this approach: featuring a large emerald drop, the tiara was worn on the forehead, as dictated by recent fashion. Current style also promoted sleeveless sheath dresses enlivened by multiple cuff bracelets, dangling pendant earrings, and long necklaces known as sautoirs and bayadères, which dropped to the waist. Even if the 1929 Stock Market Crash somewhat slowed the pace of output, Chaumet carried on. In 1931 the firm made, for Lady Bessborough, a handsomely stylized tiara evoking, on the sides, traditional interlaced reeds. That same year, King Alfonso XIII bought a simplified fleur-de-lis tiara for his wife, Queen Victoria Eugenie. In 1934 it was Baroness Cartier who took delivery of her tiara, remodeled to reflect the "Indian" fashion of the day—in a harbinger of fate, the tiara would be bought in 1937 by Lady Edwina Mountbatten, who ten years later would become the last vicereine of India. Chaumet maintained its close links to the Spanish royal family, and it oversaw the wedding gifts offered to Princess Maria de La Mercedes of Bourbon Two Sicilies for her 1935 marriage to Juan, son of King Alfonso XIII, later Count of Barcelona, by restoring certain family items and designing new ones. The very next year, Maria's brother Alfonso married Princess Alice of Bourbon-Parma and consigned a batch of old jewels to Chaumet, who lived up to its glorious past by devising three magnificent parures of, respectively, diamonds and rubies, diamonds and sapphires, and diamonds and pearls. It was the last traditional wedding-dowry commission executed by Chaumet prior to the outbreak of World War II. Subsequent economic upheavals irrevocably altered habits, and the design of tiaras declined dramatically.

Although Chaumet supplied the King of Morocco, it was not until the 2000s that a revival began, one that has continued to grow thanks to special orders and to new lines that Chaumet presents every year. Thus in 2016 the *La Nature de Chaumet* collection reinterpreted, with great sensitivity, the themes of laurel leaves, ears of wheat, and lilies. While casually knotted wheat-ears elegantly heighten a light bandeau tiara, petals of blossoming lilies, studded with rhodolite garnets and red spinels, come together to form a magical halo in a contemporary design that perpetuates Chaumet's age-old tradition of excellence.

1. Anne Dion-Tenenbaum, "The Founders: Marie-Étienne Nitot and his Son François Regnault," *Chaumet: Parisian Jeweler Since 1780* (Paris: Flammarion, 2017), p. 41.
2. Ibid., p. 43.
3. Empress Joséphine, *Correspondance 1782–1814* (Paris: Payot, 1996), p. 221.
4. Frédéric Masson, *Joséphine, Impératrice et Reine* (Paris: Editions Littéraires et Artistiques, 1905), p. 265.
5. Ibid., p. 252.
6. Frédéric Masson, *Madame Bonaparte* (Paris: Albin Michel, 1927), p. 373.
7. His father, Marie-Étienne, died in 1809.
8. Henri Vever, *La Bijouterie française au XIXe siècle* (Paris: Henri Floury, 1906), tome I, p. 52.
9. Ibid., p. 72.
10. Ibid., p. 218.
11. Isabelle Lucas, "Romantic Jewelery," *Chaumet: Parisian Jeweler since 1780* (Paris: Flammarion, 2017), p. 245.
12. Diana Scarisbrick, *Timeless Tiaras: Chaumet from 1804 to the Present* (Paris: Assouline, 2002), p. 209.
13. Grand-ducal archives, Wiesbaden, Sect. 130II/1300v.
14. Paul Claudel, "La mystique des pierres précieuses," *L'Œil écoute* (La Flèche: Folio Essais, 1990), p. 215.

FACING PAGE Robert Doisneau (1912–1994), *The Countess of Bourbon-Busset*, wearing a Lanvin gown and Chaumet tiara, at the Château de Groussay, residence of Monsieur de Beistegui, 1957.
PAGE 36 *Aigrette Impériale* tiara in the contemporary *Joséphine* collections.
PAGE 37 Chaumet's Tiara Room at 12 Place Vendôme in Paris, where the collection of historic "maillechorts" (nickel-silver maquettes) is exhibited.

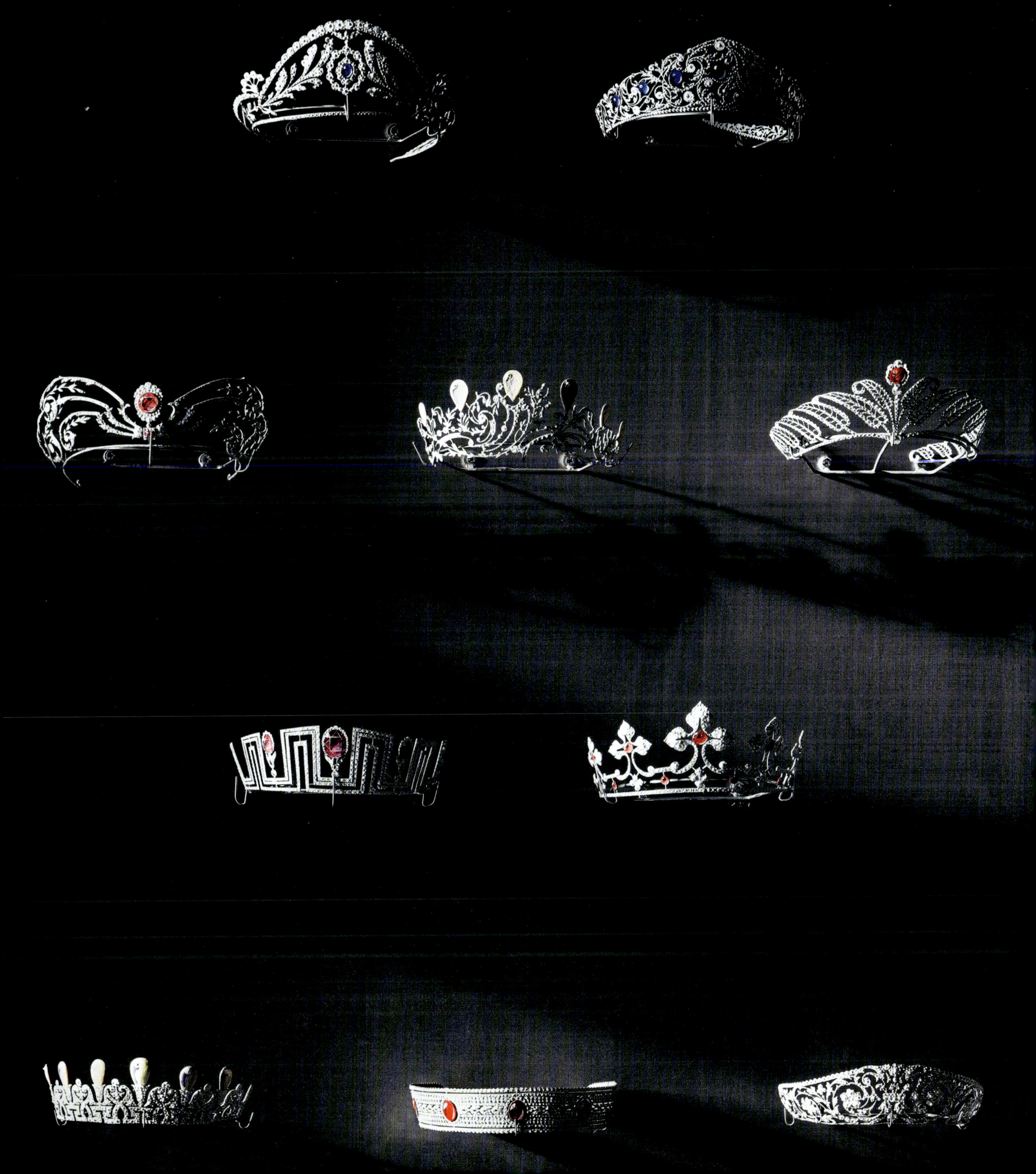

THE TIARA
DESIGN COLLECTION

Maillechort, or nickel silver, is an alloy of copper, nickel, and zinc, prized for its ductility, strength, tarnish resistance, and silvery appearance when polished. Its use by metal craftsmen grew rapidly in the first half of the nineteenth century. In his *Encyclopédie chimique*, the engineer Mathieu Villon attributed the development of the alloy to two metalworkers, Messieurs Maillot and Chorier, who combined their names to form that of this new manufacturing product.[1] Villon provides no precise date when maillechort first appeared, but a patent was registered on June 22, 1827, by the entrepreneur Philibert Maillot, active in Lyon, Quai Saint-Antoine, and a second a year later by a certain Charlier, established on Quai du Marché-Neuf on the Île de la Cité, the historical Parisian neighborhood of goldsmiths and jewelers.[2]

After succeeding his father-in-law, Prosper Morel, at the helm of the Maison around 1890, Joseph Chaumet made the nickel-silver maquette a central element of the creative process. These full-size replicas, executed mainly for head ornaments, were cut out and shaped, with touches of gouache replicating the colors of the selected stones, and sometimes even gum arabic to suggest the jewel's brilliance. This model enabled the client to try on the future tiara and make final adjustments to details. After the designer's sketch, this was the first three-dimensional materialization of the ornament. In keeping with the wishes of Nitot, who also had been keen to preserve and pass down the Maison's craftsmanship, Chaumet had a considerable number of these replicas put on permanent display at the premises in Place Vendôme in Paris, in the Salon des Modèles, thereby offering both his clientele and his employees a collection of forms and styles from which to draw inspiration. In so doing he established the tiara's preeminent position among the Maison's creations. To this day, once the tiara has been delivered, an entry for its nickel-silver replica is recorded in the inventory of heritage collections, which now contain some five hundred models. R.C.

1. Jean Girardin, *Leçon de chimie élémentaire appliquée aux arts industriel* (Paris: Fortin et Masson, 1846), p. 446; Matthieu Villon, *Encyclopédie chimique*, "Nickel" (Paris: Dunod, 1891, vol. V), p. 63; Catherine Arminjon and Michèle Bilimoff, *L'Art du métal: vocabulaire technique* (Paris: Éditions du Patrimoine, 1998), p. 31.
2. *Bulletin des lois*, no. 179, July 18, 1827, p. 172; *Répertoire du commerce de Paris, ou Almanach des commerçants, banquiers, négociants, manufacturiers, fabricants et artistes de la capitale* (Paris: Deflandre, 1829), p. 643.

FACING PAGE Joseph Chaumet (1852–1928), volume model for an ivy tiara, circa 1890. Maillechort (nickel silver), gouache, varnish. Chaumet Collection, Paris.

TIMELINE

THROUGH THE CENTURIES, YET ALWAYS THE SAME, THE MAISON CHAUMET HAS CARRIED THE NAME OF EACH SUCCESSIVE MASTER CRAFTSMAN AT ITS HELM: MARIE-ÉTIENNE NITOT, FRANÇOIS-REGNAULT NITOT, JEAN-BAPTISTE FOSSIN, JEAN-VALENTIN MOREL, JULES FOSSIN, PROSPER MOREL, JOSEPH CHAUMET, AND MARCEL CHAUMET.

1780

Marie-Étienne Nitot (1750–1809) founds his gold and silversmith company in Paris. At the time, jewelry formed part of the Corporation des Orfèvres, a guild also comprising silver and goldsmiths.

February 22, 1783

Marie-Étienne Nitot's *poinçon* or hallmark is registered with the guild of jewelers, silversmiths, and goldsmiths. Nitot works for the Court of Versailles under the direction of Aubert, Queen Marie-Antoinette's official jeweler.

1784

Nitot takes part in the valuation of the Crown Jewels in his role as a jeweler.

1790–93

As a member of the Commission des Arts, Nitot verifies the inventory of the Crown Jewels, as well as participating in various other expert valuations, including for the collected *objets d'art* belonging to Marie-Antoinette.

October 1801

Together with the jeweler Foncier, Nitot values the twelve most beautiful stones in the royal mineralogy cabinet, including the Julius II emerald, taken from the Vatican treasures following the Treaty of Tolentino in 1797.

Late 1801–early 1802

Forty-two Crown diamonds mounted, including the Regent diamond, on Bonaparte's consular sword, worn on coronation day, December 2, 1804.

1804

Cameos mounted on the Charlemagne crown for Napoleon's coronation.

1805

After mounting the jewels for the tiara commissioned by Napoleon for Pope Pius VII, including the famous Julius II emerald, Nitot's son is charged with transporting the object to the Vatican. He is introduced to Joséphine in Milan and the Maison becomes the empress's official supplier.

1806

Marie-Étienne Nitot appoints his son, François-Regnault Nitot (1779–1853), as partner. Nitot & Fils moves to 36 Place du Carrousel, Paris, which will become 2 Rue de Rivoli after the thoroughfare is redesigned.

1809
Marie-Étienne Nitot dies. The Maison is taken over by François-Regnault Nitot.

March 9, 1811
Hôtel de Gramont at 15 Place Vendôme, is purchased by Marie-Catherine Endiger, the widow of Marie-Étienne Nitot and joint heiress of the jewelry house with her three sons.

1812
The Maison opens at 15 Place Vendôme in a private mansion that will become The Ritz in 1896.

1815
François-Regnault Nitot retires, handing over the Maison's reins to his workshop manager, **Jean-Baptiste Fossin** (1786–1848).

1816
Jean-Baptiste Fossin settles at 78 Rue de Richelieu, Paris. He presents himself as "Student and successor to Nitot."

1819
A much-admired diamond bouquet of flowers wins a medal at the Exposition of Art and Technology. Fossin appears in three categories: goldsmith, jeweler, and watchmaker. As a draftsman and sculptor, he also exhibits at the salons of painting and sculpture.

1825
Fossin is appointed jeweler to their Royal Highnesses Les Enfants de France under the protection of the Duchess de Berry.

1832
Jean-Baptiste Fossin brings his son, **Jules Fossin** (1808–1869), on board as partner. On September 7 King Louis-Philippe appoints them "Fossin & Fils jeweler and watchmaker to the King."

1833
Fossin's new home is at 62 Rue de Richelieu.

1834
Jean-Valentin Morel (1794–1860) is asked by Fossin to run the lapidary workshop where he is responsible for works of art.

1845
Jules Fossin takes over the management of the Maison.

1848
Jean-Valentin Morel, winner of a gold medal at the French Industrial Exposition in 1844, opens a branch for Fossin in London at 7 New Burlington Street after his partnership with Henry Duponchel (1842–1848) is severed.

1851
The Maison takes part in the Great Exhibition in London.

1855
The Grande Médaille d'Honneur is awarded to Jean-Valentin Morel at the Paris Universal Exposition.

1861
Prosper Morel (1825-1908), son of Jean-Valentin, is appointed manager by Jules Fossin (who is heirless). The Maison is renamed "Morel & Cie (succ. Fossin)" in 1863.

1862
Prosper Morel's hallmark is officially registered.

June 17, 1875
Marie Morel, daughter of Prosper, marries **Joseph Chaumet** (1852–1928), head of the Maison's workshop.

1889
Joseph Chaumet becomes director and gives the Maison his name.

1900
The Maison wins the Gold Medal at the Paris Universal Exposition.

1901
At the International Red Cross Exhibition in St. Petersburg, Joseph Chaumet is awarded the Russian Imperial Order of St. Anne.

1902
Joseph Chaumet develops a scientific process for distinguishing a natural stone from a synthetic stone. Chaumet's laboratory for analysing and verifying precious stones and pearls is the first in France.

1903
A branch of the Maison is opened in London at 154 New Bond Street.

1907
Maison Chaumet moves to 12 Place Vendôme in the Hôtel Baudard de Sainte-James. Joseph Chaumet sets up the shops and all the services expected of a major jewelry house: colored-stone cutting; workshops for sculpture, drawing, jewelry, silver, and goldware; a mechanical workshop for manufacturing special tools; and a photography studio. Diamond cutting is carried out in Auteuil. The number of employees is about 175.

1910–11
Joseph Chaumet sends a mission to India to value the gem collections belonging to the Gaekwad of Baroda and to attract new clientele among the maharajas. Baroda and Indore will give significant commissions to the Maison until the 1930s.

February 11, 1911
Joseph Chaumet's hallmark is officially registered.

1914–18
World War I. Production slows down but Maison Chaumet does not close.

1920
There is a boom in the luxury goods and fashion market as a result of the hectic socializing during the Roaring Twenties. At the dawn of this new era, Chaumet—which has retained the loyalty of its prewar customers—meets with success once more thanks to its unfailing reputation.

1924
The New York branch opens at 730 Fifth Avenue.

1925
The International Exhibition of Modern Decorative and Industrial Arts is held in Paris. During the summer season, Chaumet is in attendance at the fashionable seaside resorts of Biarritz, Cannes, and Deauville.

1928
Joseph Chaumet dies. His son, **Marcel Chaumet** (1886–1964), succeeds Joseph. In 1920 he marries Henriette Monnet, sister of French political economist Jean Monnet, the "father of Europe."

1929–33
As a result of the 1929 Stock Market Crash, the New York branch closes, the London store moves to 22 Bruton Street, and the Paris workshops are downsized.

1930
Marcel Chaumet celebrates the Maison's 150th anniversary with an exhibition and the publication of a historical monograph by Gustave Babin entitled *Une Pléiade de Maîtres Joailliers* (A Pleiades of Master Jewelers).

1931
Chaumet takes part in the Paris Colonial Exposition.

1935
Chaumet takes part in the Brussels International Exposition.

1937
Chaumet takes part in the International Exposition of Art and Technology in Paris.

1939–45
World War II. Maison Chaumet's stock is stored in safe places, and the staff mobilized. Production slows down.

1958
Jacques and Pierre Chaumet, the sons of Marcel Chaumet, are named joint general directors.

1961
Pierre Sterlé (1905–1978) begins his collaboration with Chaumet. He sells many of his executed designs to the Maison before granting it exclusivity in 1976.

1962
Chaumet takes part in the *Dix Siècles de Joaillerie Française* (Ten Centuries of French Jewelry) exhibition at the Louvre. The Maison has subsequently participated in over thirty international shows in addition to its own exhibitions.

1970
The Arcade store in Place Vendôme is inaugurated, its modern design intended to address a wider clientele.

1979
A branch of Maison Chaumet is opened in Geneva.

1984–90
A Chaumet store opens in New York at 48 East 57th Street.

1987
InvestCorp, an international financial group, acquires Maison Chaumet, which is initially renamed Société Nouvelle Chaumet and then Chaumet International S.A.

1998
A retrospective exhibition is held at the Musée Carnavalet in Paris—*Chaumet Paris: deux siècles de créations* (Chaumet Paris: Two Centuries of Designs), March 25–June 28.

1999
Maison Chaumet is acquired by the LVMH group.

June 9, 2011
The Responsible Jewellery Council announces the certification of the French jeweler Chaumet.

2010
As a tribute to the Empress Joséphine, Chaumet's first muse, the company designs a collection in her name that evokes the tiaras that were so dear to the sovereign.

2017
A retrospective exhibition is held in the Forbidden City of Beijing—*Imperial Splendours: Chaumet, the Art of Jewellery Since the 18th Century* (April 11–July 2).

2018
A retrospective exhibition is held at the Mitsubishi Ichigokan Museum in Tokyo—*The Worlds of Chaumet: The Art of Jewellery Since 1780* (June 28–September 17).

2019
A retrospective exhibition is held at the Grimaldi Forum in Monaco—*Chaumet in Majesty: Jewels of Sovereigns Since 1780* (July 12–August 28).

Napoleon required his court to dazzle the whole of Europe. Through it, he wished to convey the image of a prosperous and glorious nation. To this effect, the emperor undertook to revive the *arts somptuaires*, luxury goods, and in so doing gave jewels a leading role: that of symbolizing the power and magnificence of his reign. During the Consulate, Bonaparte had rebuilt the venerable collection of Crown diamonds, which had been placed in storage and stolen during the Revolution. And it was Marie-Étienne Nitot, founder of Chaumet, whom he entrusted with the task of mounting on his sword the most fabulous of them all: the legendary Regent diamond.

The lavish lifestyle imposed upon the imperial court by Napoleon demanded that the ladies, Empress Joséphine, Empress Marie-Louise, the princesses of the Bonaparte and Beauharnais families, and the wives of high-ranking dignitaries and marshals, should wear jewels in all circumstances, and especially for the receptions and balls at the Tuileries Palace. This brought back the tiara which was the centerpiece of the parure, or matching set of jewels. Joséphine, who loved to adorn herself in jewelry, was a superb ambassador for the imperial pomp and splendor, and became Chaumet's first muse. The tiara came to symbolize a lady's sovereignty, an emblem of power synonymous with the crown in its civil version.

As jeweler to the royal and imperial courts of Europe, Chaumet raised the art of the tiara to new heights. As an integral part of society dress codes in the Belle Époque and the interwar periods, it displayed the wearer's rank and was an outward sign of success. But most of all, it remained the sovereign jewel, as epitomized by the tiara of the Grand Duchess of Luxembourg, exceptionally loaned for this exhibition, or that of Countess Edwina Mountbatten, last Vicereine of India.

THE TIARA

AS A STATUS SYMBOL

1 *Napoleon and Crown*

Jacques-Louis David (1748–1825)
Circa 1807
Oil on wood
H. 43.5, W. 36.1 cm
Dosne-Thiers Foundation,
Institut de France, Paris

When Napoleon came to power in 1799, neoclassicism was flourishing in France. This movement, inspired by the rediscovery of classical antiquity, breathed new life into the arts, reflecting the profound mutations of a society newly transformed by the French Revolution. When the painter David met General Bonaparte in 1797, he described the future emperor as "handsome as an ancient statue." And this was how he portrayed him circa 1807, in the guise of a Roman emperor, a Caesar crowned with laurels, in a study for an official portrait that was never executed.

Borrowing his allegorical repertory from antiquity, the emperor donned a laurel wreath in chased gold, made by the goldsmith Biennais, for his coronation in Notre-Dame Cathedral in Paris on December 2, 1804. Synonymous with victory of the ancient Greek heroes and poets, laurels were bestowed upon the great men of history to convey their glory and immortal genius. In ancient Rome, laurels were the award for a victorious general before becoming the attribute of an emperor—Napoleon's own destiny.

But for the Emperor of the French, the crown of laurels was also a reference to Alexander the Great, the most illustrious of conquerors, who introduced the *diadēma*, a more or less ornate band worn on the head as a symbol of royalty. It was this regal dimension that Napoleon would attribute to the tiara under his reign, fostering the revival of a piece of jewelry symbolizing grandeur and power. Resplendent on the heads or foreheads of empresses and princesses of the imperial family, the tiara or diadem would contribute in its own way to the spread and influence of Napoleonic pomp and splendor. K.H.

FACING PAGE

2 *Portrait of Empress Joséphine*

Studio of Baron Gerard (1770–1837)
1807–8
Oil on canvas
H. 80, W. 64.5 cm
Musée National des Châteaux de Malmaison et Bois-Préau, Rueil-Malmaison, on loan from the Manufacture de Sèvres

BELOW

3 *Bust of Empress Joséphine*

Joseph Chinard (1756–1813)
Circa 1810
Terracotta, red-ocher patina
H. 30 cm
Musée National des Châteaux de Malmaison et Bois-Préau, Rueil-Malmaison

While the classical diadem was made of gold, sometimes enriched with enamel and colored stones, the tiara of the Napoleonic period was generally set with pearls and precious stones, especially diamonds, whose brilliance enhanced the beauty of the wearer and lent her, as in this official portrait of Empress Josephine, a majestic dignity. Josephine, who had a passion for jewelry, excelled in her role as ambassador of imperial splendor, and loved to don the finest jewels from her own collection or from among the French Crown Jewels. In 1805, her favorite jewelers, Foncier and his successor Marguerite—who supplied the coronation jewels—were succeeded by the founders of Maison Chaumet, Marie-Étienne Nitot and his son François-Regnault. The empress was so struck by the tiara they had just made for Pope Pius VII that she named Nitot "Jeweler in Ordinary" and commissioned countless objects from them. Her excessive spending became a source of irritation for Napoleon, who, in an attempt to reduce his wife's expenses, in September 1808 banned nearly all tradesmen and suppliers from entering her apartments. The only one authorized to continue visiting was the "Jeweler to T.R.H. the Emperor and Empress." "The only recognized jeweler is M. Nitot," decreed the emperor, with the following proviso: "He must only be admitted once a week." K. H.

4 *Wheat-ear tiara*

François-Regnault Nitot (1779–1853)
Circa 1811
Gold, silver, diamonds
H. 6.5, W. 15 cm
Chaumet Collection, Paris

Following the proclamation of the Empire on May 18, 1804, Joséphine chose to wear diamond wheat-ears for her first appearance as sovereign of the French for the Légion d'Honneur ceremony at the Hôtel des Invalides on July 15. In her *Mémoires of 1802–8*, Madame de Rémusat wrote: "She appeared in broad daylight, attired in a robe of rose-colored tulle, spangled with silver stars, and cut very low, according to the fashion of the day. Her head-dress consisted of a great number of diamond wheat-ears. This brilliant attire, the elegance of her bearing, the charm of her smile, the sweetness of her countenance, produced such an effect, that I heard many persons who were present at the ceremony say that the Empress outshone all the ladies of her suite."

Throughout her reign, Empress Joséphine was particularly fond of wheat-ear tiaras, like this one composed of nine ears of wheat set with more than 66 carats of antique-cut diamonds mounted in gold and silver. The movement and lightness of this timeless and highly modern composition of wheat-ears create the illusion of a real-life sheaf of wheat blown by the wind.

In 1811, Napoleon commissioned several parures from Nitot that would join the Crown Jewels, including one hundred and fifty diamond wheat-ears for his new wife, Marie-Louise, to adorn her outfits and hair. The following year, a wheat-ear aigrette in emeralds and diamonds was delivered to the empress. Ever since, the ear of wheat has been a part of Maison Chaumet's naturalistic repertoire. K.H.

FACING PAGE

5 *Intaglio parure belonging to Empress Joséphine*

François-Regnault Nitot (1779–1853)
Circa 1809

Gold, silver, nicolo agate, natural pearls
Necklace L. 43.5, W. 4.5 cm. Brooch H. 3, W. 5.5 cm.
Earrings H. 4.5, W. 2 cm
Chaumet Collection, Paris

PAGES 56–57

6 *Oak leaves parure with cornelian intaglios*

François-Regnault Nitot (1779–1853)
1809

Hallmark of Antoine-Pierre Chanat
Gold, enamel, cornelian
Necklace L. 46.3 cm. Comb H. 11.3, W. 11.1 cm.
Earrings H. 4.7, W. 1.7 cm. Bracelets L. 17.6, W. 2 cm
Private collection

A passion for cameos and intaglios, in both the classical and modern styles, swept through the whole of Europe in the second half of the eighteenth century. Neoclassicism brought them back into fashion, and the stones (agate, coral, cornelian, amethyst, malachite) and carved seashells came from Italy, where the tradition of gemstone engraving had endured since the Renaissance. During the Empire, Napoleon sought to limit Italian imports, and so founded a school of hardstone carving. These cameos and intaglios, usually featuring classical figures, were sent to Paris where the jeweler Nitot mounted many of them on parures for the imperial family.

Empress Joséphine, who was a keen follower of fashion, owned a number of these parures, including this intaglio set composed of a tiara, a brooch, a pair of earrings, and a necklace. It was inherited by one of her granddaughters, also named Joséphine, who became queen consort of Sweden. While the whereabouts of the tiara are today unknown, the parure is now in the Chaumet Collection. The nicolo agate intaglios are ringed with gold and pearls. The ones in the necklace, each with a pendant, alternate with pearl-studded palmettes, a motif characteristic of the Empire period in Nitot's works. Intaglios and palmettes are joined by small chains of florets. Using a different form of intaglio, a set of cornelians reverse-carved with mythological scenes was decorated with small chains of florets, acorns, and oak leaves in mat gold. The divine symbol of the tree, representing power, wisdom, and strength, was associated with the coronation robe embroidered with bees, ears of wheat, and laurel and oak leaves. This exquisite day-parure bears the mark of Antoine-Pierre Chanat for Maison Nitot & Fils. It was among the numerous diplomatic gifts supplied by Nitot to the Service des Présents de la Cour Impériale and was given by Napoleon to Mademoiselle Clémentine Andrieux in 1809. It references, like the previously mentioned sets, the classical age, one of symbolic importance for the emperor and his family. C. V./K. H.

7 *Malachite cameo parure belonging to Empress Joséphine*

Attributed to Nitot
Circa 1810

Gold, malachite, pearls, tortoiseshell
Tiara H. 15 cm. Necklace L. 45.3 cm. Belt L. 35.5 cm. Bracelets L. 17.6 cm. Brooch H. 3.8 cm. Pendant H. 4.3 cm. Cameo pins H. 5.3 cm. Pearl pins H. 5.8 cm
Fondation Napoléon, Paris

Joséphine was a leading light in fashion and style and owned a wardrobe beyond compare. She made a splash with each of her public appearances, wearing outfits that she tastefully harmonized with her jewelry. Besides the very special parures in diamonds and precious stones used only for formal occasions and ceremonies, the empress had many "day" sets in colored gemstones that were simpler and lighter to wear, for less official use. The inventory after her death lists several malachite parures, including this one that she left to her daughter-in-law Augusta Amelia of Bavaria, wife of Eugène de Beauharnais.

Typical of the Empire style, this ensemble alternates palmettes in pearls with finely chased gold and malachite cameos of Greek gods. It is an extremely rare specimen of a set that has come down to us complete, including a tiara, pins, a necklace, a brooch, a pendant, bracelets, and a belt. K.H.

8 *Micromosaic parure*

Attributed to Nitot
Circa 1811

Gold, pearls, enamel, glass paste mosaic
Comb tiara L. 17 cm. Bandeau tiara L. 47 cm.
Necklace L. 42 cm. Earrings H. 5 cm
Museum of Decorative Arts, Prague

In 1810, Nitot supplied a micromosaic parure, a wedding gift from Napoleon to Empress Marie-Louise, which is today in the Louvre museum. Small tableaux composed with tiny tesserae of glass paste depict monuments of ancient Rome. This technique, developed in the Vatican ateliers from 1727, became very popular and soon began to be used in jewelry. It remained fashionable under the Empire and almost twenty studios were recorded in Rome in 1820. The parure in Prague's Museum of Decorative Arts features a series of micromosaic scenes of Arcadian landscapes peopled with small figures. It comprises a comb tiara, earrings, a necklace, and a bandeau tiara. In the necklace, the micromosaics framed with gold and pearls are linked together with palmettes, alternating, in the comb and the necklace, with foliage motifs topped with metal flowers with pearl centers, in turn surmounted by palmettes. Certain motifs recall the linking sections in the acrostic bracelets that belonged to Empress Joséphine. This delicately wrought day set provided an alternative to the cameos, intaglios, and colored fine stones. C.V.

9 *Portrait of Caroline Murat, Queen of Naples*

Workshop of François Gérard (1770-1837)
1810

Oil on canvas
H. 65, W. 53.5 cm
Private collection

In 1800, Napoleon's youngest sister, Caroline, married Joachim Murat, an ordinary aide-de-camp who was made a "maréchal d'empire" and "prince français" by the emperor in 1804. The young couple was granted the Grand Duchies of Berg and Cleves in 1805, and three years later, the Treaty of Bayonne brought them the kingdom of Naples. Caroline and her husband maintained a splendid court at their palaces in Caserta and Capodimonte. Always elegantly attired, Caroline owned a large collection of jewelry made up of sets that were gifts from her brother as well as pieces she commissioned herself. She often chose cameos but also loved to wear pearls and diamonds. In this portrait, she wears a sumptuous complete set in amethyst, a commonly used stone during the Empire. Nitot made an amethyst parure for Empress Marie-Louise, delivered on October 7, 1811. C.V.

10 *Amethyst and diamond parure belonging to Countess Vilain XIIII*

Circa 1810

Silver, gold, amethysts, diamonds
Necklace L. 46.4 cm. Earrings H. 5.81, W. 1.76 cm
DIVA, Antwerp – Saint-Pierre Church
Collection, Bazel

Philippe Vilain XIIII, Commandant of the Conseil Général de l'Escaut, and his wife, Baroness Zoé de Feltz, played host to the imperial couple on their visit to Ghent in May 1810. Marie-Louise was charmed by their hostess, the daughter of an Austrian diplomat, and engaged her as lady-in-waiting. At the baptism of the imperial couple's son, the Roi de Rome, Princess Aldobrandini carried the imperial baby's bonnet while Baroness de Feltz and the Comtesse de Beauvau carried the ewer and salt cellar. To commemorate this important day, Napoleon gave Zoé a splendid demi-parure of amethysts and a few months later granted her husband the title of count. The necklace of alternating large oval amethysts on fixed mounts surrounded by brilliants, linked with smaller amethysts set in gold, came with a matching pair of earrings with pear-shaped amethysts suspended on the studs. Napoleon's practice of sumptuous gift-giving is fabulously illustrated by these jewels, a fine example of the Nitots' majestic style. The demi-parure, in its original case, was bequeathed by Countess Vilain to the church council of her village in 1852, a year before her death. C.V.

11 *Two tiara designs*

Nitot
Late eighteenth–early nineteenth centuries
Graphite, watercolor
H. 14, W. 29.4 and 33.2 cm
Chaumet Collection, Paris

The Maison Chaumet Archives contain some sixty-five thousand drawings, covering over two centuries of jewelry design history—indisputably the largest collection of its kind in Europe and North America. Unchanged since the eighteenth century, the creative process begins with the drawing. In it, the designer can give free rein to his or her imagination and stylistic experimentation. It is developed in the form of sketches, and then the finished drawing, called the "gouache", is executed. Among the oldest works are these two studies for tiaras, characteristic of the neoclassicism permeating the arts in the late eighteenth and early nineteenth centuries. These drawings feature traditional neoclassical motifs, arranged in majestic pyramidal compositions playing with symmetry and steeped in allegory. They also form an iconographical repertory of the Chaumet style, almost an aesthetic manifesto.

From the Maison's beginnings, its designers have drawn inspiration from nature and sought to depict botanical species observed from life, as reflected in these drawings. In the first drawing, besides the stylized motifs of wreathes, palmettes, and calyxes, which have appeared in Chaumet's designs ever since, is a delicate, more naturalistic suggestion of lily-of-the-valley flowers. The second drawing, however, is a naturalistic composition of plant motifs, rich in symbolism. At either end of the tiara, reeds are bound together; attached to them is a cornucopia from which peach blossoms emerge, symbolizing spring. Then come bunches of redcurrants and ears of wheat, referencing Ceres, goddess of the harvest, surrounding Cupid's quiver and bow. The circle of stars around the quiver form the crowning wreath of this metaphor of Love. K. H.

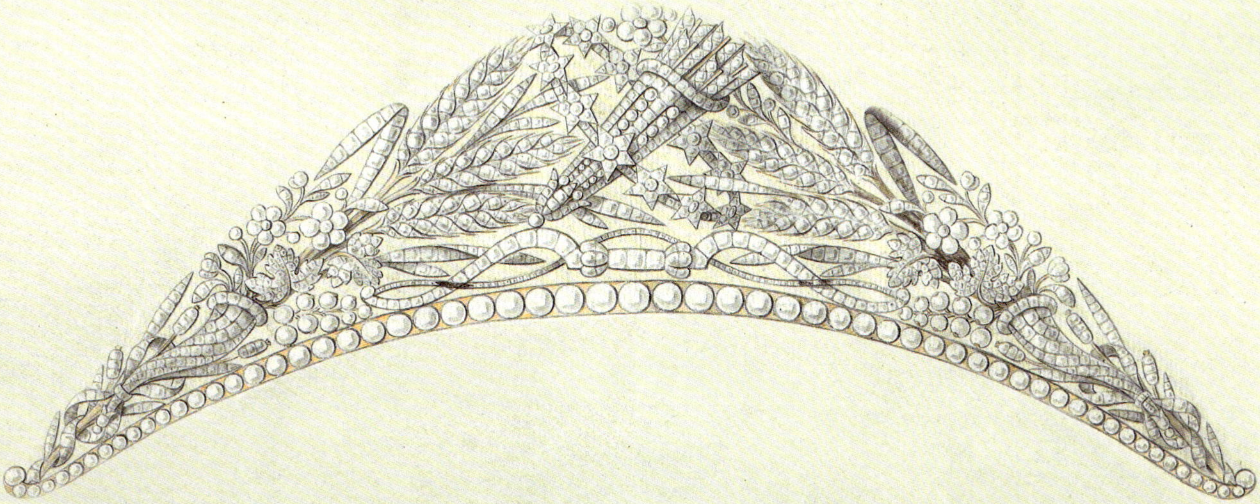

FACING PAGE

12 *Drawing of Empress Marie-Louise's ruby and diamond parure*

Nitot & Fils
1811
Watercolor, charcoal, ink, gouache
H. 66.5, W. 49 cm
Chaumet Collection, Paris

PAGES 68–69

13 *Replica of the ruby and diamond parure belonging to Empress Marie-Louise*

Nitot & Fils
Circa 1811
Gold, silver, white sapphires, zircons, garnets
Tiara H. 8.5, Diam. 19 cm. Comb H. 12.5, L. 16 cm.
Coronet Diam. 14.4 cm. Necklace Diam. 24 cm.
Girandole earrings L. 5, W. 3 cm. Bracelets L. 18 cm.
Chaumet Collection, Paris

This replica was made in the Nitot & Fils ateliers in memory of the ruby and diamond parure commission delivered to Empress Marie-Louise on January 16, 1811. A pair of bracelets, later modified for the Duchess of Angoulême and today in the Louvre Museum's Apollo Gallery, is all that is left of this parure whose whereabouts are today unknown. While the stones used in this replica—white sapphires, zircons, and garnets—are not as precious as those of the original parure, they nevertheless convey the richness and majesty of this kind of ensemble, used only for state ceremonies. As shown in a large drawing faithfully illustrating the original, this ceremonial parure included a tiara and a coronet topped with the imperial emblem, the eagle, as well as a comb, a necklace, drop earrings, a belt, and a pair of bracelets. These two creations, together with the designs for the "Charlemagne" crown, the Pius VII tiara, and the Napoleon's Imperial sword, reflect Nitot's commitment to preserving the legacy of the Maison's major works, since its beginnings, an undertaking that was faithfully pursued by Fossin, Morel, and then Joseph Chaumet. By bringing the works together and preserving them, generation after generation, and by making the most of new techniques, the archives of drawings in ink and then gouache, glass plate photography, and maillechort (nickel silver) maquettes, the four dynasties of the Maison's history forged the foundations of the Chaumet heritage. R.C./K.H.

M.E. Nitot et fils.

14 *Court dress and train belonging to Maréchale Davout, Princess of Eckmühl*

Attributed to Louis-Hippolyte Leroy (1763–1829)
1810
Tulle and ivory silk satin embroidered with gold and platinum thread
Dress L. 148, W. 33.5 cm (at the shoulders).
Train L. 240, W. 140 cm
Salle d'Eckmühl, Blocqueville Collection, Auxerre

Née Louise-Aimée-Julie Leclerc, Maréchale Davout was the sister of Général Leclerc, first husband of Pauline Bonaparte. Reputed for her thriftiness, she often embroidered her formal gowns herself, to the annoyance of her husband, who wished his wife to display the luxurious lifestyle demanded by Napoleon. Maréchal Davout asked his wife to purchase diamonds and to have at least two court gowns made. At ceremonies or receptions held at the Tuileries Palace, ladies of the imperial court were expected to wear the *robe parée*, a low-cut, high-waisted gown with a long skirt flattening the figure, more or less lavishly embroidered with silver and gold. Like Empress Joséphine, many of them placed their orders for court dress with the great *marchand de mode* Louis-Hippolyte Leroy. Joséphine found in Leroy a couturier skilled at producing gowns in her preferred elegantly light and floaty style. Leroy (whom Napoleon described as a "rag merchant"), a former wigmaker-hairdresser to Marie-Antoinette, had already been a favorite of Joséphine's under the Consulate, before becoming her official supplier during the Empire. At a time when couturier brands did not yet exist, he was the favorite dressmaker of fashionable ladies, a real celebrity whose designs were the height of fashion at courts as far away as Spain and Russia.

This gown and train, worn at the wedding of Napoleon and Marie-Louise on April 2, 1810, is among the rare ensembles that Maréchale Davout agreed to have made for her by the great Parisian couturier, in honor of the imperial wedding. In tulle and ivory silk satin, delicately embroidered in gold and platinum in a floral pattern on the central panels and in foliage garlands along the edges, it is an exceptional illustration of the magnificence of the imperial era. K. H.

15 *Portrait of Empress Marie-Louise*

Robert Lefèvre (1755–1830)
1812

Oil on canvas
H. 222, W. 153 cm
Chaumet Collection, Paris

Napoleon divorced Joséphine in 1809 because she was unable to provide him with the heir he needed for the survival of the dynasty. On April 2, 1810, he married Marie-Louise of Habsburg-Lorraine, daughter of the Emperor of Austria, who in 1811 gave birth to the long-awaited son, titled the Roi de Rome. To honor the future empress and to demonstrate the prestige of the new regime to one of the oldest monarchies in Europe, Napoleon commissioned the most magnificent of parures for the traditional "wedding basket" of gifts for the bride. Nitot rose to the challenge and continued to surpass himself, until the fall of the Empire, in supplying all of the empress's jewels, each grand ceremony providing a new opportunity for a sumptuous gift. Balzac describes this opulence in *La Paix du ménage* (*Domestic Peace*), published in 1830: "Never had the French aristocracy been so rich or so splendid. The diamonds lavishly scattered over the women's dresses… contrasted so strongly with the penury of the Republic, that the wealth of the globe seemed to be rolling through the drawing-rooms of Paris… never were diamonds so highly prized."

In this portrait, Empress Marie-Louise wears the large diamond set given to her by the emperor for their wedding. Considered the most sumptuous of the nineteenth century, this parure made by Nitot & Fils, using some of the Crown diamonds, has been lost. Few pieces of imperial jewelry have come down to us, and those that have are incomplete. Through political upheavals and changing fashions, these jewels were dismantled or transformed, or passed into private hands at the sale of the Diamonds of the Crown authorized by a law of disposal passed on January 11, 1887. However, the necklace that was a gift for the birth of the Roi de Rome in 1811 still exists. Made up of 234 diamonds weighing about 263 carats, it is today in the Smithsonian Institution in Washington, D.C. K. H.

M. E. NITOT & FILS A PARIS

16 *"Gothic" belt belonging to Empress Marie-Louise*

François-Regnault Nitot (1779–1853)
1813

Gold, natural pearls, onyx
L. 83 cm
Chaumet Collection, Paris

This belt is described as "Gothic" because it is inspired by the long belts worn by women in the Middle Ages, which dropped from the waist to the bottom of the gown. The fashion for the Gothic style under the First Empire reflects the fascination for the incipient Romantic movement. Marie-Louise herself, a keen amateur artist, executed several watercolors in 1812 and 1813 revealing an inclination for neo-Gothic fashion and architecture. Its introduction into the art of jewelry heralded the taste for historicism in the 1820s and 1830s and reveals the visionary genius of Nitot. In a bold stylistic synthesis, the jeweler managed to create a harmonious combination of rigorous and symmetrical neoclassical motifs and the attributes of Napoleonic symbolism—palmettes, bees, stars, and laurel wreaths—with interlacing and trefoil forms of medieval inspiration.

This luxuriously elegant fashion accessory was designed around an antique cameo given by the princess Pauline Borghèse, Napoleon's youngest and favorite sister, to her sister-in-law Marie-Louise. This antique gift was very much in the spirit of the times, a rare specimen dating from the Hellenistic period, depicting Apollo, god of the arts, playing the cithara after slaying the serpent Python lying at his feet. The onyx cameo, surrounded with an alternating pattern of six crescents and six ovals in carnelian set with pearls, attaches the long vertical panel to the two small side panels in chased gold studded with pearls. The forty crescent-shaped elements of the openwork vertical panel are linked together with hinges. Two thin ribbons along the sides lend flexibility to the ensemble so that it would lie neatly against the figure. K.H.

17 *Art deco tiara*

Joseph Chaumet (1825–1928)
1926

Platinum, diamonds, emeralds
H. 5.6, W. 15 cm
Grand-Ducal Collection, Luxembourg

The 1925 International Exhibition of Modern Decorative and Industrial Arts in Paris, in which the Grand Duchy of Luxembourg took part, provided a choice showcase for the French luxury industry, from which Chaumet would reap rewards. Charlotte, Grand Duchess of Luxembourg, desired a tiara with a more modern design and so turned to the jewelry house, renowned both for its traditional craftsmanship and appealing modern approach. The premises on Place Vendôme received delivery of a brooch of brilliants and a parure of turquoises and diamonds that had been bequeathed by Grand Duchess Adelheid-Marie to her granddaughter Charlotte. These were accompanied by a diamond weighing over 6 carats, unset from a gold bandeau tiara that had been worn by both Charlotte and by her sister, the Grand Duchess Marie-Adélaïde; and an emerald, weighing about 45 carats, from a brooch presented in 1859 by Emperor Franz Joseph, as a baptism gift to his godson, Prince Franz Joseph of Nassau. The workshop came up with several designs, all with the impressive oval green stone as the central ornament. The first featured a succession of fan-like motifs placed diagonally, in descending order from the central line. The second already took the final shape but included a series of circular elements flanking the large cabochon. The third, in this same shape, was enriched with diamond-studded *paragnathides* (hanging parts on each side of a tiara). This was the design, in terms of its overall organization, that most resembled that selected by Charlotte and her husband, Prince Félix of Bourbon-Parma. The piece delivered was in the purest art deco style, rising to a peak over the emerald cabochon, which was positioned above a cushion-cut diamond. On either side was a diamond-studded geometrical linear motif surrounding eight larger diamonds. Considered one of the centerpieces of the family collection, the art deco tiara was a favorite of Charlotte's; she wore it throughout her reign for numerous state visits and other important events. It also appears in many official portraits and on a series of stamps depicting the duchess, issued in June 1960. Grand Duchess Charlotte, who would play a significant role in supporting her compatriots during World War II and ensuring Luxembourg's continuing independence, remained immensely popular throughout her life. She abdicated on November 12, 1964 in favor of her eldest son, and retired to Fischbach Castle. C.V.

André Taponier (1869–1930), *Charlotte, Grand Duchess of Luxembourg*, wearing the art deco tiara made by Chaumet in 1926.

18 *Tiara with trefoils belonging to Countess Mountbatten of Burma, last Vicereine of India*

Chaumet
1934
Platinum, diamonds
Private collection

In 1928, Marie Dow, Baroness Émile de Cartier de Marchienne, made the acquisition of a tiara in the art deco style. A few months earlier, her husband had just been appointed Belgian Ambassador to the Court of St. James's. As required by British etiquette, the spouses of members of the diplomatic corps were invited to wear a head ornament at grand receptions, so it was important to respect protocol. In 1934, the baroness returned to Chaumet, desiring a new frame for her tiara. Various designs were presented and she chose a piece made up of a series of elegant scrolls surrounding trefoil motifs in the Indian style, which also adorned the top of the tiara at regular intervals. Several years later, for unknown reasons, the baroness left the tiara with Cartier, who offered it to Edwina Mountbatten for the upcoming coronation of King George VI, in 1937.

Born with the century in 1900, Edwina Ashley was the granddaughter of the 7th Earl of Shaftesbury on her father's side, and, on her mother's side, the granddaughter of the merchant banker Ernest Cassel, whose fortune she would inherit. She mingled with the best society and made the acquaintance of Louis Mountbatten, a great-grandson of Queen Victoria. She married him on July 18, 1922, forming one of the most high-profile couples in Great Britain. During World War II, Edwina Mountbatten spared no efforts raising funds for the British Red Cross and the St. John Ambulance Brigade, while Mountbatten served in the Royal Navy. But Edwina found in India the role of her life, when, at her husband's side, between 1947 and 1948, she became the last vicereine of India. She developed a close friendship with Nehru and a great fondness for the nation. She wore the tiara at the coronations of King George VI and Queen Elizabeth II to dazzling effect. Edwina and Louis Mountbatten had two daughters, Lady Patricia and Lady Pamela. The tiara passed to one of them, and was put up for sale in 2002. C.V.

Madame Yevonde (1893–1975), *Edwina, Countess Mountbatten of Burma*, wearing her Chaumet tiara at the coronation of King George VI, 1937.

19 *Fuchsias tiara belonging to Princess Hedwige of Bourbon-Parma*

Joseph Chaumet (1825–1928)
1919

Platinum, diamonds
H. 7, W. 18 cm
Chaumet Collection, Paris

The La Rochefoucauld family maintained close links with the house of Chaumet, and Armand, Duke of Doudeauville, naturally approached the jeweler for the commission of wedding gifts for his daughter Hedwige, who was to marry Prince Sixtus of Bourbon-Parma on November 12, 1919. Sixtus was the well-connected son of Robert I, Duke of Parma and the Infanta Maria Antonia of Portugal. He was also the brother of Zita, Empress of Austria, and of Félix, husband of Charlotte, Grand Duchess of Luxembourg. This royal union, appearing so soon after World War I, was widely covered in society magazines. Articles described the trousseau and weddings gifts, among which a sumptuous tiara took pride of place. It had a motif of open-petaled fuchsias with suspended graduated drop diamonds. Nine drop-shaped finials crowned the jewel. The stones were set in trompe l'oeil, a tried-and-tested technique often used by Chaumet; it sought to create the illusion of a single stone by gathering several diamonds in a discreet pear-shaped mount. The tiara combined both the taste for a naturalistic style, in which the Maison had always excelled, and a sophisticated stylization that heralded the emerging art deco style. As fashion dictated at the time, Princess Hedwige wore the tiara as a bandeau at the wedding of Prince Leopold of Belgium and Princess Astrid of Sweden, in Brussels, on November 10, 1926. Later, she would wear it higher on the head, as a crown. Princess Hedwige died in 1986, but her daughter Isabelle had already been using the tiara for many years. The princess, who married Count Roger de La Rochefoucauld, with whom she had four sons, wore the tiara regularly for receptions at the grand ducal court, in Luxembourg. It is today one of the centerpieces of the Chaumet Collection. C.V.

Princess Isabelle, Countess of La Rochefoucauld (sole daughter of Prince Sixtus and Princess Hedwige of Bourbon-Parma) wearing the fuchsias tiara during a reception at the court of Luxembourg.

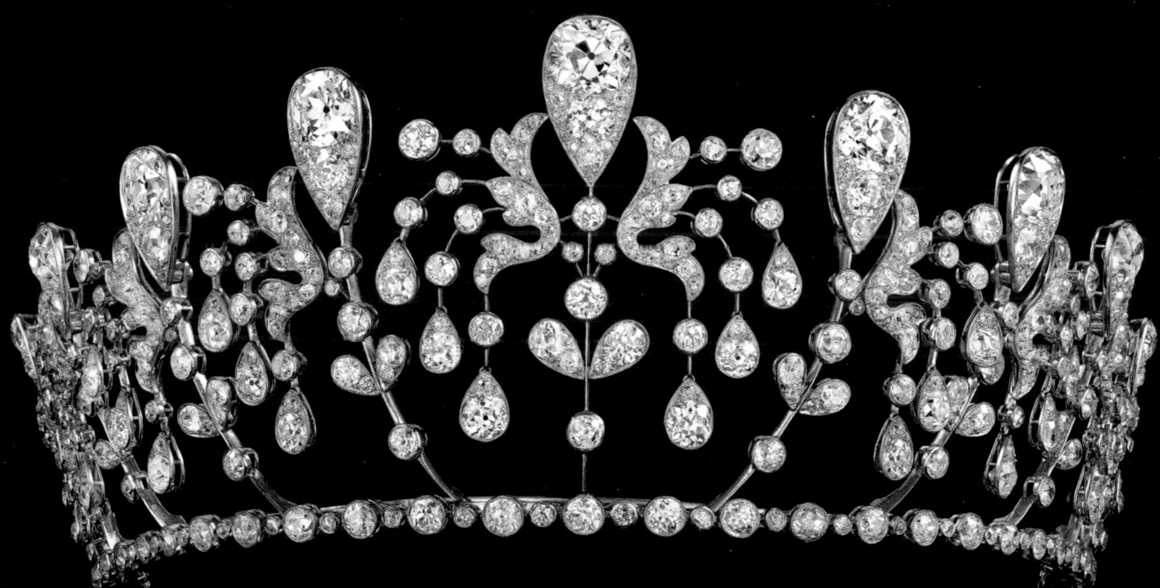

20 *Baroque pearl tiara*

Chaumet
Circa 1930
Platinum, natural pearls, diamonds
H. 6, W. 15 cm
Chaumet Collection, Paris

This tiara with simple forms showcases a set of pearls of remarkable quality. Twenty-six baroque pearls form an elegantly majestic halo, while the extremely rare central pearl weighs 75 grains. The tiara was loaned on several occasions to Princess Isabelle of Orléans-Braganza, Countess of Paris. Born in Eu at the family château inherited from King Louis-Philippe, she always loved returning to Normandy. The eldest daughter of Prince Pedro de Alcântara of Orléans-Braganza and Countess Elisabeth Dobrzensky of Dobrzenicz, Isabelle married her distant cousin, Prince Henri, future Count of Paris, on April 8, 1931, in Palermo at the Orléans Palace. The couple had eleven children, and resided in Belgium, Morocco, and Portugal, before returning to France on the repeal of the Law of Exile in 1950. Titled Madame la Comtesse de Paris, the princess, who embodied royal dignity very naturally, became a popular figure in Parisian society, well liked for her affable nature and good humor. She enhanced festive occasions with her elegance and throughout her life showed impeccable taste in the choice of her attire, placing her trust in the great couturiers and the hairdresser Alexandre. She had access to a number of head ornaments, historic pieces from the family collection, but was always fond of this diamond and pearl tiara, which she often borrowed from Chaumet to wear for official portraits, grand receptions, and family gatherings. C. V.

Princess Isabelle d'Orléans-Braganza, the Countess of Paris, wearing the baroque pearl tiara.

A splendid custom that goes back to the seventeenth century, the *corbeille de mariage,* or wedding basket of gifts, was a popular tradition in the nineteenth and twentieth centuries, before being replaced by social practices more in tune with the times. Originally, the term *corbeille* designated a fabric-covered wicker basket in which the groom's gifts to his bride were placed. It carried the promise of a felicitous wedding and a prosperous marriage, echoing the ambitions of great alliances that united titles and fortunes. The tiara was, for aristocratic families in the nineteenth and twentieth centuries, the centerpiece of the wedding basket, and over time has become the symbol of the union of love.

Joséphine received a wedding basket when she married the young General Bonaparte in 1796, but her future husband's still-modest means did not permit it to contain precious jewelry. As emperor, however, Napoleon would shower the empress with the finest parures and jewels conveying his feelings for the woman of whom he would say, "She has embellished fifteen years of my life." The acrostic bracelets forming the first names of Joséphine's childen, Eugène and Hortense, now in the collection of Queen Margrethe II of Denmark, are a fine and moving example. In 1806, Nitot supplied the jewelry parures for the weddings of Eugène de Beauharnais and Augusta Amelia of Bavaria, of Stéphanie de Beauharnais and the Grand Duke of Baden, and of Jérôme Bonaparte and Catharina of Württemberg in 1807, before delivering the lavish basket of gifts for the wedding of Empress Marie-Louise in 1810.

For aristocratic families, the value of the wedding basket depended on the nature of the bride's gifts, which were exhibited from the morning of the signature of the marriage contract until the day of the ceremony. Newspapers would describe the sumptuous jewels and tiaras in their society columns. Many of the three thousand five hundred or so tiaras designed by Chaumet have been for weddings, and the tradition endures today. An extension of the ancient bridal crown, the tiara remains the incarnation of marriage, the tangible sign of an eternal commitment, and the crowning symbol of love.

THE TIARA

LOVE’S CROWN

21 *Portrait of Empress Joséphine*

Antoine-Jean Gros (1771–1835)
1808–9

Oil on canvas
H. 215, W. 140 cm
Musée Masséna, Nice

Far from the ceremonial formality of the imperial court, Joséphine poses here in the privacy of her Château de Malmaison, a place symbolizing elegance and a pleasant and delicately sensual style of living. In the background of the composition, the view extending into Malmaison's English garden, with its river and hazy silhouettes of the Temple of Love and the Marly Aqueduct, evokes the extensive landscaped estate developed by the empress. The album on which her hand rests, entitled *Flore de Malmaison*, an unknown work, recalls Joséphine's passion for botany and the hundreds of species that she had acclimatized in a hothouse near the château.

But this painting is also a family allegory, with the painter seeking to portray the empress as a caring and loving mother. Joséphine contemplates the bust of her son, Prince Eugène, from whom she has received a letter—the envelope at her feet is marked *À sa Majesté l'Impératrice et Reine, le Prince Eugène*—while the porcelain vase next to her bearing her initial, J, contains a bouquet of hydrangeas, an allusion to her daughter, Hortense, Queen of Holland. Eugène and Hortense, her children from her first marriage with Alexandre, Viscount of Beauharnais, who was executed in 1794, were adopted by Napoleon, out of true affection and also in the hope that the children would inherit the throne. This portrait, completed in 1809, the year of the divorce imposed for reasons of state, is a poignant symbol of the future of the discarded empress, for whom Malmaison and her children's love were the last refuge. K. H.

22 *Pair of acrostic bracelets belonging to Empress Joséphine, forming the names Eugène and Hortense*

François-Regnault Nitot (1779–1853)
Circa 1806

Diamonds, precious and colored fine stones
L. 19.1 and 19 cm
Collection of the Danish Royal Family's Entailed Estate for Movables

Acrostic bracelets, a classic type of sentimental jewel, were very fashionable under the Empire. Inspired by the principles of poetic composition, the initials of the stones with which the bracelet was set formed a message—of love, commemoration, a first name: the possibilities were endless. These pieces in the Danish royal collections belonged to Empress Joséphine and refer to her two children. The first bracelet, set with six stones and 147 diamonds forming floret links, make up the name Eugène (emerald, uniaxial crystal, garnet, emerald, nicolo, emerald). The second, on a similar model, has eight stones and 157 diamonds making up the name Hortense (hessonite, opal, ruby, turquoise, emerald, nicolo, sapphire, emerald). The pair, which Eugène inherited when his mother's estate was divided after her death in 1814, bore the inventory number 78 and was valued at 1,680 francs. It was passed down to his daughters Amélie, Empress of Brazil, and Joséphine, Queen of Sweden. When Amélie died childless, the bracelets were reunited and passed to one of Joséphine's granddaughters, Princess Louise of Sweden, who, in 1869, married the future King Frederik VIII of Denmark, great-grandfather of Queen Margrethe II. C.V.

FACING PAGE

23 *Joséphine's wedding basket*

Anonymous
1796
Silk, silver, copper, papier mâché
H. 44, W. 54 cm
Musée National des Châteaux de Malmaison et Bois-Préau, Rueil-Malmaison

The term *corbeille de mariage* (wedding basket) originally referred to a fabric-covered wicker basket used to contain gifts to the future bride from her husband-to-be. It was garnished more or less lavishly, depending on the couple's social status, with jewelry, fans, and precious objects, lace and embroidered fabrics, Indian cashmeres, chiffon blouses, handkerchiefs, stockings, bonnets, gloves, and other such finery. Joséphine was the recipient of such a basket on the occasion of her wedding to the young General Bonaparte in 1796. Elegantly simple in style, this oval-shaped, six-sided container has a lid topped with a copper sphere and on which the initial J for Joséphine was once embroidered in silver. Set on a small pedestal mounted on a rectangular base, the basket is entirely covered with white silk that has deteriorated over time, and is embroidered with beads and leaves in silver thread and edged with fluting and egg-and-dart motifs. Two copper rings serve as handles. Conserved in the imperial family collections, Joséphine's wedding basket was donated to the Château de Malmaison in 1979 by Prince and Princess Napoleon. K. H.

BELOW

24 *Ring belonging to Joséphine with the initials JNB*

Anonymous
Circa 1796
Gold, enamel
Diam. 20 mm
Musée du Louvre, Paris, Department of Decorative Arts, on permanent loan to the Musée National des Châteaux de Malmaison et Bois-Préau, Rueil-Malmaison

This ring is thought to have been given by General Bonaparte, in 1796, the year of his marriage, to the woman he renamed Joséphine and of whom he would later say, "I can tell you, she was the woman I loved most." This jewel is not listed in the queen's inventory after her death, because it was probably given to her daughter, Queen Hortense, who is thought to have passed it to her son, Napoleon III. Empress Eugénie gave it to Dr. Hugenschmidt, her personal physician, who donated it to the Louvre in 1930.

This gold ring with blue enamel has the letters JNB (Joséphine Napoleon Bonaparte) cut out in the center, with scrolling on either side, and the inscription "amour sincere" (true love) on a blue enamel ground around the outer edge. In its simplicity and its dedication, this small ring is reminiscent of the sentimental jewels popular in the eighteenth century. K. H.

25 *Wedding certificate of Joséphine and Napoleon*

Copy of the entry in the marriage register of March 9, 1796, dated February 17, 1829

H. 37, W. 26 cm

BNP Paribas, Historical Archives, Paris

On March 9, 1796, because Napoleon was in the midst of preparations for his next military campaign—the famous First Italian Campaign, which would bring him fame and glory—his wedding with Joséphine was scheduled for the evening. Bonaparte arrived at the town hall of the 2nd arrondissement in Paris two hours late, at 10 p.m., for a short civil ceremony that was not followed by a reception. The registration of this hasty marriage—the banns had been published less than four months after the couple first met, in the autumn of 1795—was full of irregularities. The date of birth, title, and address of the young general, whose name was still spelled in the Corsican manner, "Napolione," were all incorrect. He aged himself by eighteen months, and "Marie-Joseph-Rose de Tascher de la Pagerie" was rejuvenated by four years, making the pair practically the same age. Napoleon, who was obliged to leave Joséphine two days later for the battlefields, expressed his love for her in passionate letters that have become famous: "I have not spent a day without loving you; I have not spent a night without clasping you in my arms... without cursing the glory and ambition which keep me from the heart of my very being."

The copy, issued in 1829, of the future imperial couple's marriage license is the only trace of this ceremony, the original having been lost in a fire during the 1871 Commune of Paris. The room where Napoleon and Joséphine were married remains unchanged in what is known as the Hôtel de Mondragon, which today houses the headquarters of the BNP Paribas bank. As for the religious ceremony, it wasn't until December 1804, on the eve of the coronation, that Cardinal Fesch could bless the couple in the Chapelle des Tuileries. K.H.

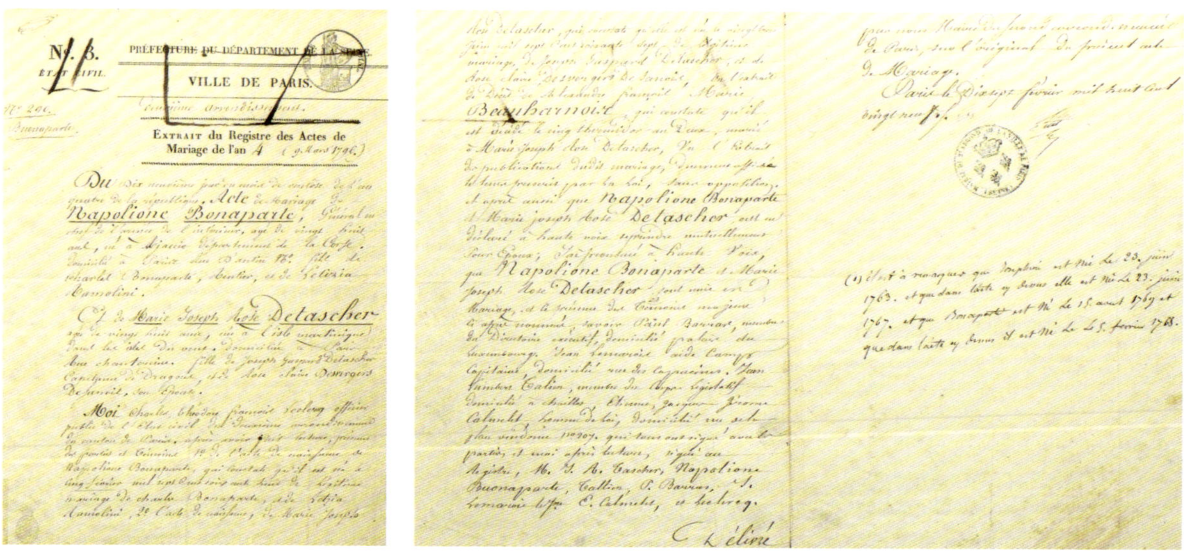

PRÉFECTURE DU DÉPARTEMENT DE LA SEINE

VILLE DE PARIS.

EXTRAIT du Registre des Actes de Mariage de l'an 4 (9 Mars 1796.)

N°. 8.

ÉTAT CIVIL.

N°. 290.

Buonaparte.

PRÉFECTURE DU DÉPARTEMENT DE LA SEINE.

VILLE DE PARIS.

deuxième arrondissement.

EXTRAIT du Registre des Actes de Mariage de l'an 4 (9 Mars 1796.)

Du dix neuvième jour du mois de ventôse de l'an quatre de la république, Acte de Mariage de Napolione Bonaparte, Général en chef de l'armée de l'intérieur, agé de vingt huit ans, né à Ajaccio département de la Corse, domicilié à Paris rue d'antin N°. fils de Charles Bonaparte, Rentier, et de Letizia Ramolini.

Et de Marie Joseph Rose Detascher agé de vingt huit ans, née à l'isle martinique dans les isles du vent, domiciliée à Paris rue chanteraine. fille de Joseph Gaspard Detascher Capitaine de Dragons, et de Rose claire Desvergers Desanois, son Epouse.

Moi Charles Théodore françois Leclercq officier public de l'Etat civil du deuxième arrondissement du canton de Paris, après avoir fait lecture, présence des parties et Témoins, 1°. de l'acte de naissance de Napolione Bonaparte, qui constate qu'il est né le cinq février mil sept cent soixante huit de légitime mariage de charles Bonaparte, et de Letizia Ramolini, 2°. l'acte de naissance, de Marie Joseph

26 *The Religious Marriage of Napoleon I and Marie-Louise in the Salon Carré at the Louvre, on April 2, 1810*

Georges Rouget (1783–1869)
1810
Oil on canvas
H. 190.5, W. 182 cm
Musée National des Châteaux de Versailles et de Trianon, Versailles

On April 2, 1810, the religious wedding ceremony of Napoleon and Marie-Louise took place in the Salon Carré of the Louvre, transformed into a chapel by the architects Percier and Fontaine. The moment depicted here is Cardinal Fesch's blessing of the imperial couple, who hold each other's right hand, surrounded by the princes, princesses, and dignitaries of the court. Inspired by Jacques-Louis David's painting of the coronation, on which he had worked, Rouget reprised its solemnity while imparting a sense of intimacy that was impossible to achieve in the huge painting of the coronation at Notre-Dame, by narrowing the scene to a smaller group of figures in a pool of light at the altar. The work has a real monumentality, however, framed to include the high galleries, giving the illusion of a place of worship. The split-level composition contrasting the dark and empty upper half with the crowded and light-filled lower half emphasizes the majesty of a painting celebrating a union that carried the future of the Empire.

The lavish lifestyle that Napoleon imposed upon the imperial court dictated that the ladies of the court should wear jewelry in all circumstances, not least at important ceremonies like this one. Adorning the heads of Marie-Louise and the princesses assembled behind her are the magnificent tiaras made by Nitot. K. H.

A

FACING PAGE

27 *Case for the malachite parure belonging to Empress Joséphine*

Empire period

Wood, leather, satin, velvet
H. 25.5, W. 46, D. 7.8 cm
Fondation Napoléon, Paris

BELOW

28 *Jewelry box belonging to Empress Joséphine*

Early nineteenth century

Wood, leather, white satin
H. 8.7, W. 24, D. 17.5 cm
Musée National des Châteaux de Malmaison et Bois-Préau, Rueil-Malmaison

Jewelry boxes are inseparable from their precious contents and yet are often forgotten or ignored. The first of these two boxes (facing page), in red morocco, and whose curious shape recalls that of Napoleon's hat, is the original case for Empress Joséphine's malachite parure. Bearing the inscriptions "A [below a crown], n°50 PARURE MALACHITES ENTOUREE DE PERLES" (Malachite Parure Surrounded with Pearls), it was probably passed down to Augusta Amelia, wife of Prince Eugène, who owned several other jewelry pieces in cases with the same type of inscription.

The second box (below) is semi-cylindrical in form and covered with red morocco leather. The lid is decorated with a gilded garland frieze and bears the monogram PB—perhaps for Pagerie-Bonaparte—on a diamond of green morocco leather. In the front, the inscription "S.M. L'IMPERATRICE ET REINE. MALMAISON" (H.M. The Empress and Queen. Malmaison) highlights the illustrious provenance of this item. C. V./K. H.

29 *Jewelry box*

Jean-Baptiste Claude Odiot (1764–1850)
Circa 1810

Silver-gilt, silk
H. 25, W. 30, D. 21 cm
Hallmarks of Jean-Baptiste Claude Odiot ("B./J.C./O."); sterling silver assay mark (1809–19)
Palácio Nacional da Ajuda, Lisbon

This precious box in the Empire style, resting on the spread wings of four doves, was made at the workshops of Jean-Baptiste Claude Odiot, official supplier to Napoleon and his family. The silversmith received the great honor of making the cradle for the Roi de Rome, today in the Imperial Treasury, Vienna. This box is richly decorated; the long sides depict cupids holding up a garland of laurel leaves encircling the lock. Foliage motifs extending from their bodies entwine a tripod decked with flowers, between corner pilasters. The other sides of the box feature an arrangement of scrolls, trophies, and garlands, a motif that is repeated on the lid topped with two winged, spinning putti in high relief. A foliate frieze in low relief runs along the edge of the lid and base of the box. Empress Marie-Louise owned a similar jewelry box made by Odiot after a design by Garneray circa 1810. An almost identical box was also commissioned by Czar Alexander I, which was perhaps given to Queen Hortense, daughter of Joséphine, who owned a very similar one. C.V.

30 *Portrait of Stéphanie, Grand Duchess of Baden*

Workshop of François Gérard (1770–1837)
1806

Oil on canvas
H. 105, W. 140 cm
The Prince's Palace Collections, Monaco

Like many members of the imperial family, Stéphanie de Beauharnais posed for the painter François Gérard. Born in 1789, she had been abandoned by her father, a distant cousin of Joséphine's. She was taken in by Napoleon and Joséphine in 1803 and officially adopted by them in 1805. This gave the emperor an extra card to play to ensure his dynasty, and he decided to marry Stéphanie to Charles, future Grand Duke of Baden. In keeping with his policy of ostentation, he wished his adopted daughter to dazzle in her new country and commissioned a lavish wedding basket of gifts from Nitot. In her *Mémoires*, Mademoiselle Avrillion, first lady-in-waiting to Empress Joséphine, recounts that Stéphanie received "a superb parure of diamonds and many jewels of exquisite taste." In this portrait, the Princess of Baden wears a matching set of emeralds and diamonds from the jeweler's workshops, including the necklace and earrings that are today in London's Victoria and Albert Museum. Stéphanie, Grand Duchess of Baden is a direct ancestor of Prince Albert of Monaco. C.V.

FACING PAGE

31 *Portrait of Augusta Amelia of Bavaria*

Joseph Karl Stieler (1781–1858)
1824–25
Oil on canvas
H. 73, W. 60 cm
Musée National des Châteaux de Malmaison et Bois-Préau, Rueil-Malmaison

BELOW

32 *Bust of Augusta Amelia of Bavaria*

Joseph Chinard (1756–1813)
Circa 1810
Terracotta, red-ocher patina
H. 29.5 cm
Musée National des Châteaux de Malmaison et Bois-Préau, Rueil-Malmaison

To strengthen his political and military position, Napoleon imposed alliances with European dynasties on his family, notably with those of the states of southern Germany: Bavaria, Baden, and Württemberg. In January 1806, the wedding of Eugène de Beauharnais and Augusta Amelia of Bavaria, daughter of Maximilian Joseph, elector of Bavaria, provided the opportunity for a sojourn at the imperial court of Munich, which François-Regnault Nitot was invited to join. On the emperor's orders, Nitot supplied the bride's jewels, for the sum of 821,969 francs, including a diamond parure that alone was worth 300,000 francs. Eugène wished to present his future wife with a gift of his own, and asked the jeweler to suggest various jewels. In the end it was Joséphine who found him the ideal gift: a tiara that she had had made resembling one worn by the famous actress Mademoiselle Georges of Comédie-Française, and that Nitot had just delivered to her.

The marriage was a happy and prosperous one. Augusta Amelia reigned in Milan with her husband, who was named Viceroy of Italy from 1805 to 1814. After Waterloo, the couple went into exile in Bavaria, and were granted the Duchy of Leuchtenberg. The royal marriages of their children make Empress Joséphine the ancestor of most of the reigning dynasties of Europe today.

In these portraits painted and sculpted some fifteen years apart, Augusta Amelia wears a set of pearls, almost certainly the same. The necklace in Stieler's portrait, probably a gift from Joséphine under the Empire, had detachable pearls that could be worn in the hair attached to bands or to braids, as in Chinard's small bust. K.H.

33 *Double-strand pearl necklace known as "Leuchtenberg"*

Attributed to Nitot
Early nineteenth century
Gold, silver, diamonds, pearls
L. 43 cm
Private collection

This double-strand pearl necklace featuring seven detachable pear-shaped pearls mounted on diamond-set caps is exceptional in both its beauty and its provenance. Inherited from Empress Joséphine, it belonged to Augusta Amelia of Bavaria, wife of Prince Eugène de Beauharnais, and was passed down to their daughter, also named Joséphine, who became Queen of Sweden in 1844 through her marriage to the Crown Prince Oscar of Sweden, the future Oscar I.

The pearls of the Crown were considerably enriched thanks to Nitot, initially to satisfy Joséphine, who was very fond of them and who owned several sets, and later to honor Napoleon's second wife, Archduchess Marie-Louise of Habsburg-Lorraine. For their wedding in 1810, Nitot supplied a parure consisting of two necklaces, a comb, strands to wear in the hair, earrings, and bracelets, completed in 1881 with a 408-pearl sautoir and a 297-pearl tiara. Pearls were rare and it took time to collect the required number, so it wasn't until 1812 that the coronet of 1,233 pearls was added to the ensemble. The largest pearl in this parure was given pride of place in the center of the tiara. Weighing 346,27 grains on its sale by Nitot, the size of a pigeon's egg, it was the largest known pearl in Europe. Named the Regent on its sale in 1887 with the Crown Jewels, this pearl, sometimes also known as the "Napoleon," was acquired by Fabergé. It was reset as a pendant, a gift from Prince Nikolai Yusupov to his daughter Zinaida, who gave it to her son Felix in 1914 on the occasion of his marriage to Irina of Russia. K.H.

34 *Pair of wristwatches belonging to Princess Augusta Amelia of Bavaria*

Nitot & Fils

1811

Gold, emeralds, pearls

L. 19,5, W. 3 cm

Chaumet Collection, Paris

This pair of wristwatches, the first known of its kind in the history of Chaumet, was commissioned for Princess Augusta Amelia of Bavaria in 1811. It followed the principle of symmetrical bracelets worn as a pair, items found in all of the jeweler's parures under the First Empire, and features a composition of back-to-back scrolls studded with emeralds and pearls, similar to that of the bracelets in the ruby and diamond parure belonging to Empress Marie-Louise, today in the Louvre Museum. One of the watches shows the hour, the other the date. Their original case, in red morocco leather, bears the initial A beneath the crown of Augusta Amelia, along with the number 33, in reference to an inventory of jewelry that has not been found. K.H.

BELOW

35 *Portrait of Catharina of Württemberg, Queen of Westphalia*

Workshop of François Gérard (1770–1837)
Circa 1810
Oil on canvas
H. 56, W. 49 cm
Royal Collection of the Netherlands, The Hague

FACING PAGE

36 *Book-shaped frame containing portraits of Jérôme Bonaparte, King of Westphalia, and Catharina of Württemberg*

Nitot & Fils
Miniatures by Jean-Baptiste-Jacques Augustin (1759–1832)
1809
Gold and enamel
Inscribed "Etienne Nitot et Fils, Jouailliers Bijoutiers de L.L.M.M. l'Impératrice, le Roi et la Reine de Westphalie à Paris"
H. 6.8, W. 5.0, D. 1.1 cm
Albion Art Collection, Tokyo

On August 22, 1807, in Paris, Catharina, daughter of King Frederick I of Württemberg and Princess Augusta of Brunswick-Wolfenbüttel, married Napoleon's youngest brother, Jérôme Bonaparte, who had just been proclaimed King of Westphalia. Honored by the arrival of a royal in the family, the emperor wished to show due respect for the princess's rank and commissioned Nitot to make a sumptuous set of jewels. In article seven of the marriage contract, it is stipulated that: "His Majesty the Emperor of the French, King of Italy, and His Imperial Highness the Prince Jérôme undertake to give Her Imperial Highness the Princess Frédérique Catherine Sophie Dorothée jewels and stones to the value of three hundred thousand francs."

Among the jewelry supplied, a sumptuous diamond parure drew the most attention. The princess wore it at the wedding ceremony that was held at the Tuileries Palace and painted by Jean-Baptiste Regnault. The tiara looks similar to the one worn by the young queen in this portrait. Made up of a series of palmette fleurons with linking sections of laurel leaves, it magnificently illustrates the grand style developed by Nitot under the Empire. It came with a matching comb, which was worn at the back of the head in the chignon, girandole earrings, and a diamond necklace containing a miniature of her husband, King Jérôme. She wore a high-waisted gown and puff sleeves topped with a Medici collar. King Jérôme awarded Nitot a warrant as official supplier, and placed orders with him for numerous decorative objects: snuffboxes, monogrammed boxes, and book-shaped frames in chased gold to house miniatures, as in this example, dating from 1809, containing portraits of Jérôme and Catharina. C.V.

37 *"À tact" watch belonging to Jérôme Bonaparte, King of Westphalia*

Abraham-Louis Breguet (1747–1823),
Nitot & Fils
1809

Inscribed on the inside "Breguet No 615"
Gold, silver, diamonds, pearls, enamel
Diam. 5.5 cm
Fondation Napoléon, Paris

Synonymous with luxury, elegance, innovation, and technical perfection, the watches made by Breguet were highly prized under the Empire by all the rulers and dignitaries of Europe. Nitot and Breguet—who probably met at the court of Versailles—would produce some exceptional jewelry watches together. Among these precious pieces were "à tact" watches, which could be read both in the traditional manner, by opening the lid, and also in the dark. By touching a diamond-studded arrow on the lid, one could tell the time by feeling which of the twenty-four markers around the dial it was pointing to, with the hours indicated by diamonds and the half-hours by pearls. The Duke of Wellington related how "à tact" watches were used by gentlemen to tell the time in a tactful manner in the company of ladies, without having to remove their watch from a pouch. But Joséphine herself owned one, delivered in 1800, which she later gave to her daughter, Queen Hortense (in the Breguet Collection). The "à tact" watch belonging to Jérôme Bonaparte, acquired on December 14, 1809, has the same gold and blue enamel case with a diamond arrow. K.H.

38 Clover *brooch belonging to Empress Eugénie* (second version)

Jules Fossin (1808–1869)
1853

Gold, silver, diamonds,
translucent green enamel
H. 3.7 cm, W. 3.4 cm
Private collection

Emperor Napoleon III, who reigned over France from 1852 to 1870, chose to marry a woman he loved and respected rather than a "woman unknown to me, with whom an alliance would have had advantages mixed with sacrifices." Breaking with the custom of European courts who married among themselves, the emperor chose a young Spanish woman, Eugénie de Montijo, who was not a member of a royal dynasty. Because the future empress had been delighted at the sight of a small clover covered with dew during a walk in the grounds at Compiègne, France, Napoleon III acquired from Fossin a trefoil-shaped brooch in emeralds and diamonds. Eugénie also owned another version of the jewel in enamel and diamonds. She was very fond of this delicate piece, symbolizing her growing romance with the emperor, and wore it constantly, at the center of her bodice, as here in this formal portrait painted in 1853.

The symbolism of the three-leaf clover refers to the Christian Trinity and Empress Eugénie, who was very pious, was no doubt mindful of this allusion, but it was because of its sentimental value that she kept it all her life. Considered an engagement present by the imperial court, Eugénie's *Clover* brooch was a modest gift in comparison with the sumptuous pieces that had been made by Chaumet for sovereigns since the early nineteenth century. As such, it encapsulates a magical moment and symbolizes the beauty of a blossoming love. K. H.

Édouard-Louis Dubufe (1819–1883), *Portrait of Empress Eugénie* (detail), shown wearing her *Clover* brooch, 1853. Oil on canvas. Musée National du Palais du Château de Compiègne, Compiègne.

FACING PAGE AND PAGES 116–17

39 *Empress Eugénie's wedding missal, a gift of Princess Mathilde*

Jules Fossin (1808–1869)
1853

Gold, silver, enamel, pearls, emeralds, rubies, brilliants, velvet, parchment
H. 13.8, W. 10.2, D. 3.5 cm
Private collection

The Countess of Montijo, mother of the future Empress Eugénie, was a long-standing customer of Fossin, Nitot's successor since the fall of the First Empire, and naturally took her daughter to the jeweler's. By strange coincidence, the two women resided at 12 Place Vendôme, in 1851 and 1852, where Joseph Chaumet would open the Maison in 1907. Among their orders recorded during those two years are a diamond wreath of nine jasmine flowers and the supply of 169 pearls for a six-strand necklace, and a snake bracelet. On January 6, 1853, the Countess of Montijo placed a more symbolic order for "two wedding rings in plain polished gold, in one Eugénie Louis Napoléon, in the other Louis Napoléon Eugénie." Napoleon III asked for Eugénie's hand on January 15, the civil ceremony took place on January 29 in the Throne Room at the Tuileries Palace, and the religious service was held the next day, on January 30, in Notre-Dame Cathedral in Paris.

The empress wore a gown with a basque bodice of white velvet and a tunic of Alençon lace beneath a veil, with a double wreath of orange blossoms and brilliants. Witnesses noted that she shimmered with diamonds: "The tiara, the belt, etc., were indeed those worn by Marie-Louise at her coronation but the three great Parisian jewelers, Fossin, Lemonnier, and Moïana altered and added details that lent them new splendor even while retaining their overall style." Among the orders placed with Fossin for the wedding were bracelets, shoulder and bodice brooches, and a parasol mount in green enamel studded with diamonds. Fossin also supplied the wedding missal that Princess Mathilde, cousin of the emperor, gave to Eugénie, which contained the illuminated text of Napoleon III and Eugénie's wedding mass. The binding bears a crowned eagle and the double initial of Eugénie beneath her crown. K. H.

Lasset
uns anbeten in Ewig-
keit das heiligste Sa-
crament.
Lobet den HErrn alle Ge-
schlechter, lobet ihn alle Völker.
Lasset uns.
Denn seine Barmherzigkeit ist
befestigt über uns, und des Herrn
Wahrheit währet ewiglich
Lasset uns.
Ehre sei dem Vater und dem
Sohne und dem heiligen Geiste
Lasset uns.
Wie es war im Anfang jetzt und im-
er und zu ewigen Zeiten. Amen
MESSE
DU MARIAGE.

40 *Full-length portrait of Princess Mathilde, study for Baptism of the Imperial Prince*

Thomas Couture (1815–1879)
1856
Oil on canvas
H. 92, W. 73 cm
Musée National du Château de Compiègne, Compiègne

Princesse Mathilde, daughter of Jérôme of Westphalia and Catharina of Württemberg, almost married her cousin, Louis-Napoleon Bonaparte, the future Napoleon III, before the latter's political affairs brought about the termination of their engagement in 1836. Her marriage in 1840 to the wealthy Russian count Anatoly Demidov, Prince of San Donato, an unhappy union due to her husband's brutal and uncouth behavior, ended in a separation granted by personal decision of Czar Nicholas I in 1847. The princess, who was independent, charismatic, and intelligent, taking responsibility for her tumultuous love affair with Count van Nieuwerkerke, Superintendant of the Fine Arts, was one of the most high-profile women of the Second Empire. In 1852, Napoleon III granted her a private mansion at 24 Rue de Courcelles in Paris, where Mathilde would host a renowned literary and artistic salon. It was attended by the Goncourt brothers, Flaubert, Sainte-Beuve, and Théophile Gautier, the sculptor Carpeaux, as well as the painters Hébert, Baudry, and the Giraud brothers.

This sketch, part of the series of studies executed for the *Baptism of the Imperial Prince*, a painting that remained unfinished, shows Princess Mathilde in all her sovereign dignity. She wears the head parure supplied by Fossin in 1842, made up of a crown with seven diamond finials that could be replaced by pearls, and a diamond tiara with a central stone that could be replaced with another stone such as an opal, sapphire, or emerald, or with a diamond eagle.

Throughout her life Mathilde presented herself as Napoleon I's niece and she wore the eagle tiara, a symbol of her dynastic membership, until the end of her life. K.H.

41 *Carnation tiara commissioned by Madame Henri de Wendel*

Joseph Chaumet (1852–1928)
1905

Platinum, diamonds
H. 7, W. 19 cm
Private collection, courtesy of Albion Art Jewellery Institute, Tokyo

This tiara was commissioned in 1905 for Galliane de Wendel, the wife of Henri de Wendel, a wealthy French industrialist, on the occasion of the wedding of their son François to Odette Humann. The Wendels, a powerful family belonging to a famous dynasty of steelmakers, were typical of Chaumet's clientele during the French Belle Époque.

Moving away from the Romantic models of the previous century, Joseph Chaumet reinterpreted naturalistic flower motifs, in keeping with the influences of Art Nouveau, while drawing inspiration from the compositions of the jeweler Augustin Duflos, published in his *Recueil de dessins de joaillerie* of 1767, who had designed several stomachers and brooches in the form of carnation bouquets. As a symbol of passion and true love, the choice of the carnation was an appropriate motif for a jewel celebrating a wedding. In this tiara, Chaumet offers a boldly stylized depiction of a delicate and wild nature, in the form of twelve carnation flowers bending as if blowing in the wind, an effect heightened by the flexible frame. Here once again, it is the skill of the jeweler that enables the full expression of the designer's creativity. The central diamond, a 19.56-carat, antique-cut brilliant, can be detached and worn as a pendant. K. H.

42 *Rosette tiara*

Joseph Chaumet (1852–1928)
1920

Platinum, diamonds
H. 5.5, W. 17 cm
Private collection

This significant tiara was commissioned in 1920 for the wedding of Leopoldo Sáinz de la Maza y Gutiérrez-Solana, Count of La Maza and Maria Cristina Falcó y Álvarez de Toledo, Countess of Frigiliana, daughter of Manuel Felipe Falcó y Osorio, Duke of Fernán Núñez. The jewel was part of a lavish wedding basket of gifts supplied by Chaumet that also included a long ruby and diamond necklace. The family of the bride, loyal customers of the Maison, entrusted the jewelry workshops with some older jewels to be transformed into a new piece. The tiara was composed of a series of rosettes, a common element in the design vocabulary of classical antiquity, appropriated by the neoclassical movement and the decorative arts. The rosettes are encircled by two arcs, suggesting one of the jeweler's own motifs, often used in the designs of this period: the *écu compté* or overlapping disc motif. The workshops opted for the millegrain setting, in vogue since the very beginning of the twentieth century, which enhances the stones by catching the light and heightening their sparkle. C. V.

43 *Emerald tiara belonging to the Countess de Pimodan*

Joseph Chaumet (1852–1928)
1925

Platinum, diamonds, emeralds
H. 5, W. 18 cm
Private collection

Delivered on January 12, 1925, this platinum tiara is made up of a wide graduated band of alternating panels decorated with a stylized palmette and panaches, each of which is topped with a drop emerald fleuron. This piece could be worn on the forehead, as was fashionable at the time, and was a wedding gift to Madeleine Pillet-Will, great-granddaughter of Hyacinthe Pillet-Will, regent of the Banque de France, granddaughter of the banker Frédéric Pillet-Will, owner of the Château-Margaux vineyard, and daughter of Frédéric Pillet-Will and Antoinette Foy. In 1925, she married Georges Rarécourt de La Vallée de Pimodan, Duke of Rarécourt and Count de Pimodan, thereby becoming a member of the French aristocracy. Madeleine would inherit another diamond bandeau-style tiara by Chaumet, which had been made for her mother in 1920. C.V.

FACING PAGE

44 *Laurel leaf tiara*

Joseph Chaumet (1852–1928)
1920

Gold, silver, diamonds
H. 5.6, W. 15.5 cm
Private collection

This diamond tiara with a laurel-leaf motif, supplied in mid-November 1920 for a family wedding, was designed with stones belonging to the client and perfectly illustrates the stylistic codes and craftsmanship of Maison Chaumet in the early twentieth century. Its references to nature are typical of the Maison, with branches of laurel leaves and berries—a nod to the classical laurel wreath—floriated scrolls, and calyxes evoking the fuchsia flower. Here they are highly stylized and perfectly symmetrical, in keeping with the art deco conventions of the time. The pear-shaped element in the center of the piece uses the trompe l'oeil technique. K. H.

PAGES 128–29

45 *Scrollwork tiara belonging to the Marquise de Talhouët*

Joseph Chaumet (1852–1928)
1908

Gold, silver, diamonds
H. 6, W. 16 cm
Chaumet Collection, Paris

Supplied by Joseph Chaumet in 1908, probably for the marriage of Yvonne, eldest daughter of the Marquis René-François de Talhouët-Roy, to Jean de Nicolaÿ, this tiara is, among the pieces in the antique jewelry collections, one of the best examples of classicism in the work of the Maison in the latter years of the Belle Époque. Its remarkably balanced and symmetrical design, based on the stylized acanthus leaf—the principal ornamental motif in the history of Western art since antiquity—is fully inspired by the plant scrolls used in architecture and the decorative arts almost without interruption since the Renaissance. R. C.

46 *Wavescroll tiara*

Joseph Chaumet (1852–1928)
1909

Diamonds, platinum
H. 4.5, W. 16 cm
Private collection

In the "Society" section of its June 19, 1909 issue, *Le Gaulois* reported: "The Count and Countess of Heeren held an elegant reception in their rooms on Avenue Hoche on the occasion of the signing of their daughter's wedding contract," going on to list the illustrious contributors to the wedding basket, including the Duke and Duchess of Luhnes, the Duke and Duchess of Rohan, the Duke and Duchess of Guiche, and the Countess of Béarn. This tiara, which can be converted into a choker, was delivered a few days previously to Mademoiselle de Heeren, and perfectly illustrates the stylistic transition operated by Maison Chaumet after 1900. While retaining the kokoshnik form and richly ornamental details that correspond to Belle Époque tastes, the rigorous symmetry of its overall design heralds the principles of the art deco style in the strength and simplicity of the wavescroll pattern, stripped of the foliage that usually accompanies it. R.C.

47 *Tiara belonging to Princess Henckel von Donnersmarck*

Attributed to Joseph Chaumet (1852–1928)
Circa 1900

Platinum, gold, silver, emeralds, diamonds
H. 9, W. 17.6 cm
Qatar Museums

Count Guido Henckel von Donnersmarck amassed a huge fortune from his steelworks and coal mining businesses. His first wife, Esther Lachman, a famous courtesan better known as La Païva, received generous gifts from him. Chaumet mounted two yellow diamonds on a brooch for her: an 82.48-carat pear-shaped stone attached to a 102.54-carat cushion-cut stone. Three years after La Païva's death in 1884, the count married a Russian aristocrat, Katharina Wassilievna de Slepzow, and, soon, Chaumet was receiving more commissions, including a corsage ornament with two lizards holding a 34-carat ruby. The genesis of this tiara, dating from the turn of the twentieth century, when the count became a prince, is complex. The central band, resting on a garland of laurel leaves, is formed of eleven cushion-cut yellowish diamonds alternating with pairs of lily-of-the-valley. Crowning the diamond-set base are eleven pear-shaped emeralds. These are traditionally believed to come from the private collection of Empress Eugénie, wife of Napoleon III. When the empress went into exile, she left the Crown Jewels behind, but took away her large private collection. To finance her daily life, she deposited part of the collection with Christie's, who held a sale in 1872, consisting of 123 lots including some twenty-five polished pear-shaped emeralds. It is probable that the set of stones crowning this tiara was acquired at this extraordinary auction, and is a fitting reminder of the empress's love for emeralds. C.V.

48 *Tiara and necklace from the wedding basket of the Duke and Duchess of Montellano*

Joseph Chaumet (1852–1928)
1891–1926

Gold, diamonds, turquoises
Tiara H. 5.3, W. 15.5 cm.
Necklace L. 21, W. 12.8 cm
Private collection

In 1891, Chaumet was commissioned to make the gifts for the wedding basket of Dona Carlota Maximiliana de Escandón y Barrón. The daughter of Antonio de Escandón y Garmendia, an immensely wealthy Mexican banker and industrialist who lived in Paris, she married Don Felipe Falcó, 8th Duke of Montellano. At the time, it was customary to exhibit wedding baskets of gifts to the guests and members of the public, who were invited to file past the magnificent jewelry creations before the ceremony. It was a way for those who had commissioned the pieces to display their social status to all those present. The new duchess received a turquoise and diamond parure made up of a tiara, a necklace, and two brooches, an *esclavage* necklace of rubies and brilliants, a single-strand pearl necklace, a monogrammed fan, an openwork mirror, several rings, a brooch, and a triple-strand pearl necklace. The tiara and the necklace exhibited here were made from this historic parure delivered in 1891. Although they have been transformed, they illustrate the lavishness of wedding baskets at the time. The design is based on the bowknot, a symbol of marriage. C.V.

BELOW

49 *Bowknot corsage ornament with garlands and tassels*

Joseph Chaumet (1852–1928)
1913

Platinum, rubies, diamonds
H. 10.5, W. 10.5 cm
Faerber Collection

Recalling the eighteenth-century fashion for using fancy adornments enhancing women's hair, corsage, sleeves, stomacher, gown, and skirts, the bowknot, quite apart from its obvious symbolism, is a central motif in Chaumet's designs, notably in brooches and corsage ornaments. Here, defining the lines of a remarkably fluid design, two foliate scrolls support the calyx of a flower suggesting a fuchsia, symbol of ardent love. From this, garlands of graduated diamonds, supported by a fine, mobile mesh, cascade naturally. The bold arrangement of the composition's two rubies, unequal length of the graduations, and lively sparkle produced by the millegrain technique on the ridges of the platinum structure all serve to temper the perfect symmetry of the upper part, producing a vitality that was characteristic of the Maison's designs under Joseph Chaumet. R.C.

FACING PAGE

50 *Ribbon bowknot tiara*

Joseph Chaumet (1852–1928)
Circa 1890

Gold, silver, diamonds, pink topazes
H. 5, W. 16 cm
Chaumet Collection, Paris

From declaration to promise of marriage, from engagement to wedding, a jewel is the most dazzling proof of sentimental attachment. From its beginnings, Maison Chaumet has expressed the sentiment of love in its jewelry creations; indeed, love is the principal subject of most of its designs, through the play of traditionally symbolic forms and motifs. In keeping with Belle Époque taste for charming but symmetrical arrangements, this small tiara features ribbon bowknots and floral garlands, representing so many ties, as symbols of love—a sentiment also suggested by the topazes' pink hue. R.C.

FACING PAGE

51 *Large bowknot brooch*

Joseph Chaumet (1852–1928)
1922

Gold, silver, diamonds, fine pearls
H. 7.5, W. 8.5 cm
Chaumet Collection, Paris

BELOW

52 *Art deco bowknot brooch*

Joseph Chaumet (1852–1928)
Circa 1925

Diamond, rubies, rock crystal
W. 8, H. 1.6 cm
Chaumet Collection, Paris

A few years before the 1925 International Exhibition of Modern Decorative and Industrial Arts in Paris, which would usher in the art deco style, Maison Chaumet began progressively to move toward symmetry, balance, and more simple designs, without abandoning the liveliness that infused its style. The rigorously modular, mirrored arrangement, strong, taut lines, and alternation of stylized leaves and natural pearls with irregular shapes make this large bowknot brooch one of the most striking examples of the stylistic transition that took place under Joseph Chaumet in the 1920s, at a time when the Maison excelled particularly in its work with pearls, of which Chaumet was an eminent specialist.

Dating from just a few years later, the small diamond and ruby bowknot—whose design, geometrical composition, arrangement, and use of materials such as rock crystal perfectly suggest the folds of a light ribbon trimmed with lace—is an illustration of the stylistic evolution achieved by the designers of the Maison. R.C.

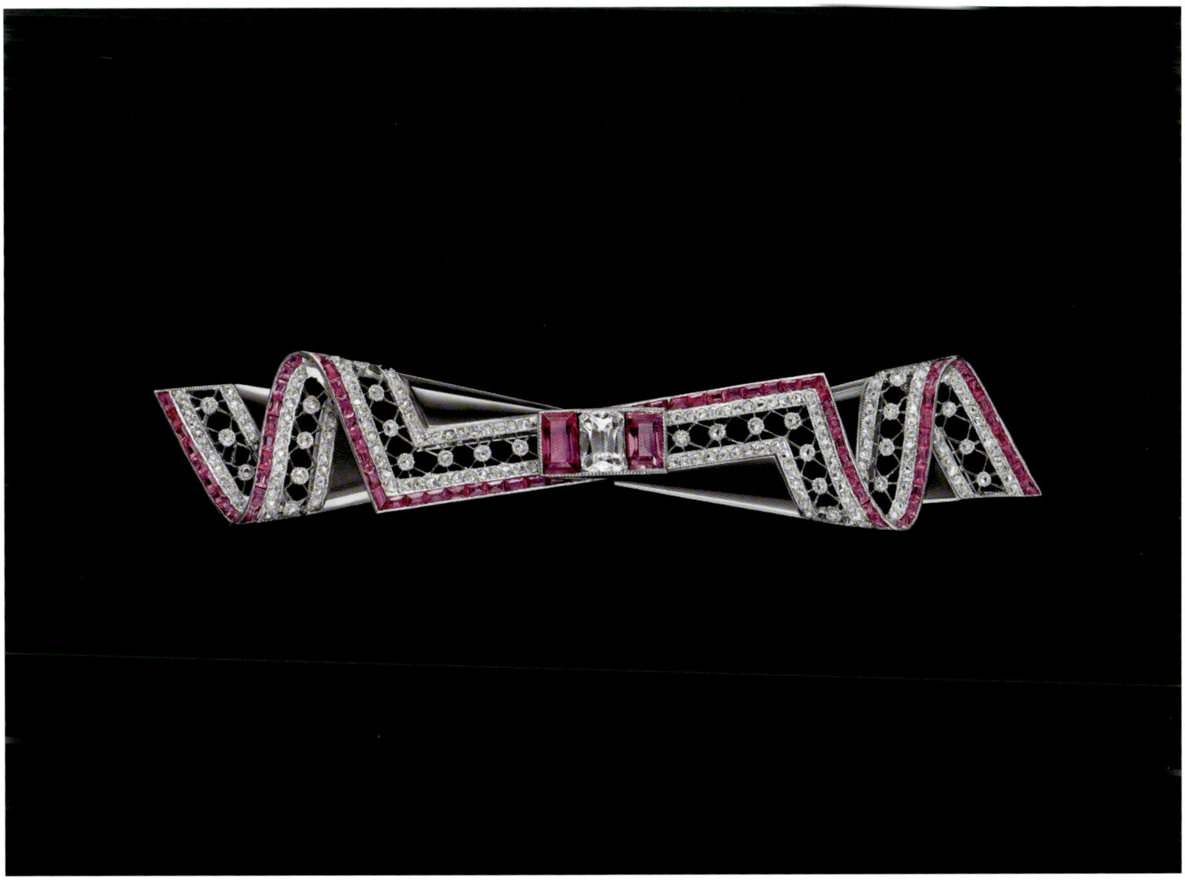

53 *Articulated choker known as the "Rohan" choker*

Joseph Chaumet (1852–1928)
1906

Platinum, diamonds
H. 6, L. 33 cm
Chaumet Collection, Paris

The articulated choker was an indispensable fashion accessory at the turn of the twentieth century. Always worn with an evening gown or ball gown, the only garment in a woman's wardrobe with a neckline cut low enough to reveal the top of the shoulders, the choker, also called a "dog collar" by jewelers in the early twentieth century, is a type of necklace that is generally broad and worn quite high on the neck. This one is flexible so as to mold itself to the shape of the wearer's neck.

It was commissioned in 1906 by Alain-Charles-Louis, 11th Duke of Rohan, as a wedding gift for his daughter-in-law Anne de Talhouët-Roy who married his son Jehan de Rohan-Chabot. This lacy piece of jewelry was exceptionally light and flexible and fully articulated, thanks to ever-improved technical innovations in the design of the frames. The delicate diamond-studded mesh was executed using the "knife-wire" technique in platinum, a metal whose intrinsic resistance enabled the frame to be made as thin and flexible as possible. R. C./K. H.

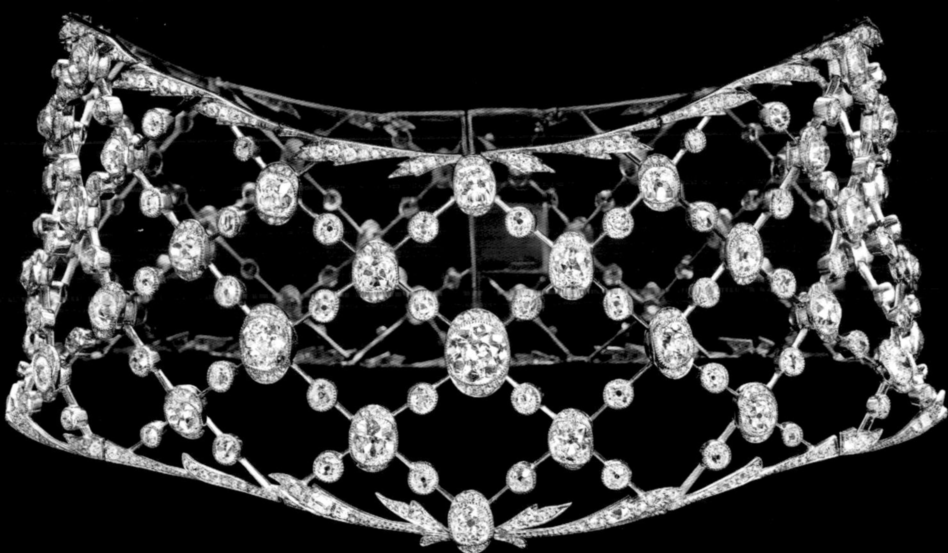

54 Links *choker transformable into a bandeau tiara*

Joseph Chaumet (1852–1928)
1910–22

Yellow gold, silver, diamonds, sapphires
L. 31.5, W. 2.5 cm
Chaumet Collection, Paris

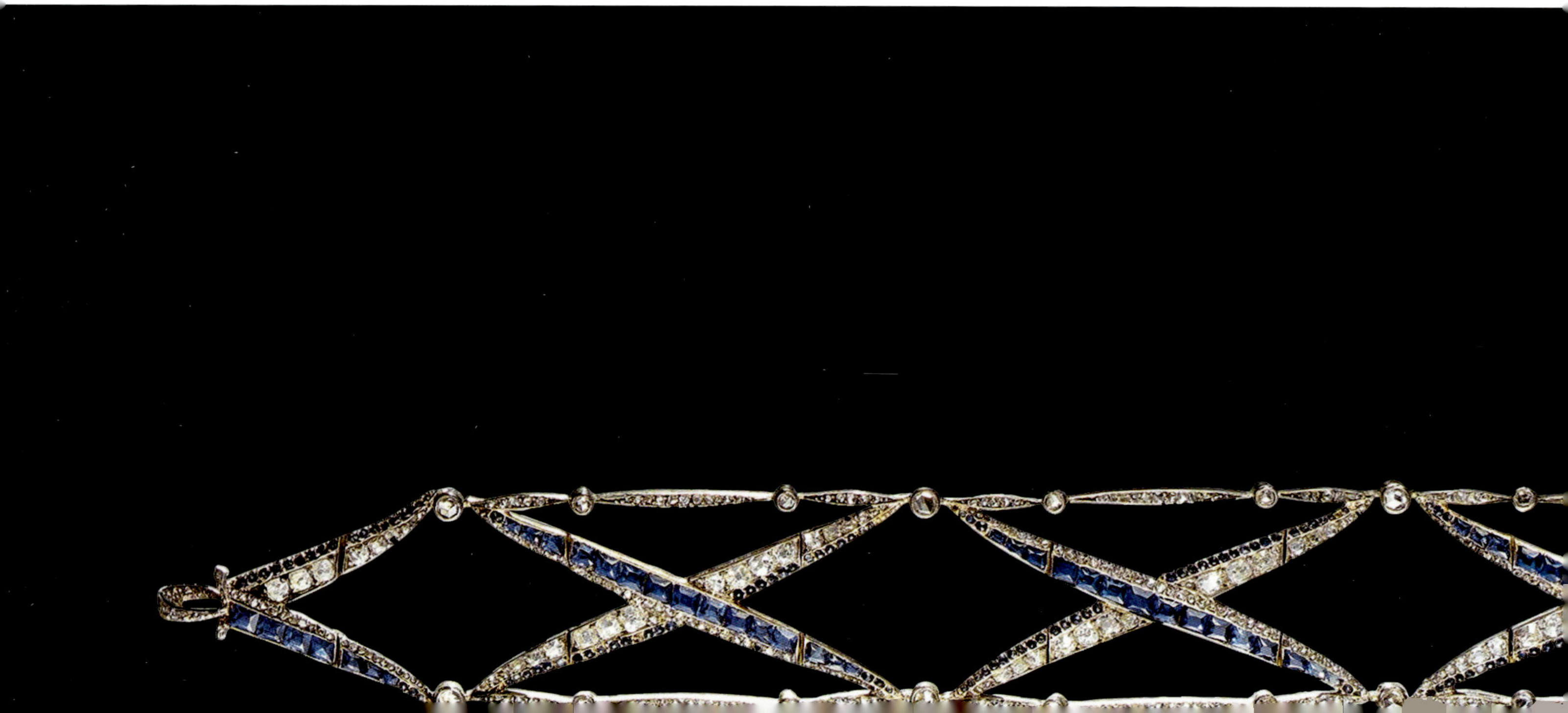

After the bowknot motif, inherited from the eighteenth century, in this choker a simple link serves to symbolize sentimental attachment. Delivered in 1910, it was converted in 1922 into a "Bandeau X sapphires & diamonds." With its very simple, graphic design, this bandeau tiara, worn on the forehead, corresponded to the new taste for clear forms. Inspired by an interwoven ribbon, the link becomes here, for Chaumet, the most beautiful of metaphors, that which tells of love in all its forms. K. H.

It is rare to be able to tell the story of a jewel that remained in the same family for more than two hundred years. It is even rarer to see it come down to us after its passage through the centuries. The "Leuchtenberg" and "Crèvecœur" tiaras are magnificent and evocative examples, attesting to the clientele's loyalty to the jeweler. The tiara occupies a special place in the history of the great aristocratic families, as an object that carries an identity. The centerpiece of the family's heritage, it symbolizes the transmission of memory, a family transmission that goes hand in hand with the concept of transforming a jewel to meet modern tastes, from generation to generation, in keeping with fashions and trends. Through its intimate knowledge of the jewels it supplies, maintains, and transforms for weddings and family legacies, Maison Chaumet has over time become a witness to the important events in the lives of those for whom it works. Updating old jewels, repairing them, and modifying them: these are among the primary missions of a great jeweler.

As an exceptional work of craftsmanship, the tiara can also, from its conception and upon the client's request, change its shape and function to suit the times and fashions. The concept of the transformable jewel, offering its owner the possibility of modifying it and turning it into a different piece, is at the heart of Chaumet's creative approach, which can accommodate any flight of fancy or bold design feature. A necklace can become a tiara; a bandeau tiara a choker or a bracelet. Certain parts can be detached to serve as a different piece of jewelry; the central feature of a tiara or a necklace can be converted into a corsage ornament, a brooch, or a pendant; a long sautoir can be divided into a pair of bracelets. A spectacular example is the 1935 navettes tiara with five detachable elements that can be turned into a necklace using a system of removable rings. Besides transformability, the ultimate in sophistication is replaceable gemstones. The *Keroüartz* tiara, convertible into a necklace, has seven pendants onto which either seven diamonds or seven pear-shaped pearls with diamond-set calyxes can be attached as desired.

In the diverse ways in which it can be worn, jewelry is an art of metamorphosis: the metamorphosis of a jewel, which, through its multiple transformations, escapes the passing of time and fashions; and the metamorphosis of the woman who makes the most of these creative possibilities.

TRANSMISSION

AND TRANSFORMATIONS

55 *Portrait of Empress Marie-Louise, Duchess of Parma, Piacenza, and Guastalla*

Giovanni Battista Callegari (1787–1855)
Circa 1820
Oil on canvas
H. 162, W. 108 cm
Galleria d'Antiquariato Datrino, Castello di Torre Canavese

On the fall of the Empire, Marie-Louise returned to Austria, her native land, and stayed at Schönbrunn Palace. In May 1815, the Great Powers of the Congress of Vienna granted her the duchies of Parma, Piacenza, and Guastalla. She only left for Italy on March 7, 1816, making her official entry into her new domain on April 18. She would reign over the duchies until 1847. In this portrait, besides the Grand Cordon sash of the Constantinian Order of Saint George, of which she was Grand Master, she wears the necklace that Napoleon gave her on the birth of the Roi de Rome. It was made by Nitot and on Marie-Louise's death was passed down to Archduchess Sophie, mother of Emperor Franz Joseph, and was inherited by her descendants until 1948. The young duchess also wears a pair of girandole earrings and a tiara with palmettes under arches with alternating bee and star motifs in between. This jewel, directly referencing the decorative vocabulary of imperial neoclassicism, corresponds to a design (pages 148–49) conserved in the Chaumet Archives. It is possible that this tiara was part of a parure made by Nitot for the empress in 1810 with diamonds brought from Vienna. The parure also included a comb, a pair of earrings, two necklaces, and a belt. As they were part of her private collection, it is not surprising to see her wearing these jewels after the fall of the Empire. They appear in various portraits of Marie-Louise, as Duchess of Parma. Although she had already decided not to visit Napoleon on the island of Elba, the former empress nevertheless holds a laurel wreath and wears a tiara in which palmettes, bees, and stars implicitly refer to her husband's fallen Empire. C. V.

56 *Design for a bandeau tiara with palmette, bee, and star motifs for Empress Marie-Louise*

Pen and black ink, traces of graphite on laid paper
H. 21.3, W. 32.5 cm
Inscription in brown ink, bottom center
"Dessin à moitié, du bandeau en Brillants fait pour marie-Louise femme de Napoléon Ier/no 2"
("Half-drawing of bandeau in brilliants made for Marie-Louise wife of Napoleon I/no. 2")
Chaumet Collection, Paris

Brillants fais pour marie Louise femme de Napoleon 1er
No 2

FACING PAGE AND PAGES 152–53

57 *Wheat-ear tiara known as the "Crèvecœur," transformable into a corsage ornament*

François-Regnault Nitot (1779–1853) and Joseph Chaumet (1852–1928)
1810–1910

Gold, diamonds
H. 18, W. 16.5 cm
Private collection

PAGES 154–55

58 *Series of four studies showing the transformations of the "Crèvecœur" tiara*

Joseph Chaumet (1852–1928), drawing studio

Graphite pencil, black ink, white gouache
H. 12.7, W. 17; H. 11.5, W. 19.3;
H. 16.8, W 21.8; H. 14.1, W. 24.8 cm
Chaumet Collection, Paris

When Jean de Crèvecœur placed an order in November 1910 for a "wheat-ear tiara transformable into a corsage ornament" as a gift for his future wife, Mademoiselle Martine Hottinguer, it was his family's history that he was passing on in this jewel. It is traditionally believed that the six diamond wheat-ears were a gift of Napoleon to Otto, Count of Mosloy, a Strasbourg diplomat, to thank him for having negotiated the contractual terms of his marriage to Marie-Louise of Habsburg-Lorraine in 1810. The emperor was generous in his gifts and this fine one was intended for the Countess of Mosloy, América Francès (known as Fanny), née Saint John de Crèvecœur. She was the daughter of Michel-Guillaume de Crèvecœur, a Normandy-born aristocrat who lived in the United States, famous in Europe for the publication in 1782 of his *Letters from an American Farmer*. Napoleon's gift of wheat-ears, an allusion to Fanny's father's deep interest in agriculture, would be passed down to the Crèvecœur heirs for four generations before being brought back to Chaumet in 1910 to be remounted on a tiara for Jean de Crèvecœur's fiancée.

Chaumet's drawings and archives enable us to retrace the original commission for and transformation of these jewels: from the deposit of the stones, recorded and photographed, to the studies for a new design and the production of a more fashionable piece. The "Crèvecœur" tiara, a striking combination of neoclassical naturalism and the flowing lines of art nouveau, can be entirely dismantled and converted into a corsage ornament typical of the Belle Époque. It has come down to us unchanged since 1910, still in its original case containing the structural elements and tools for its transformation. K. H.

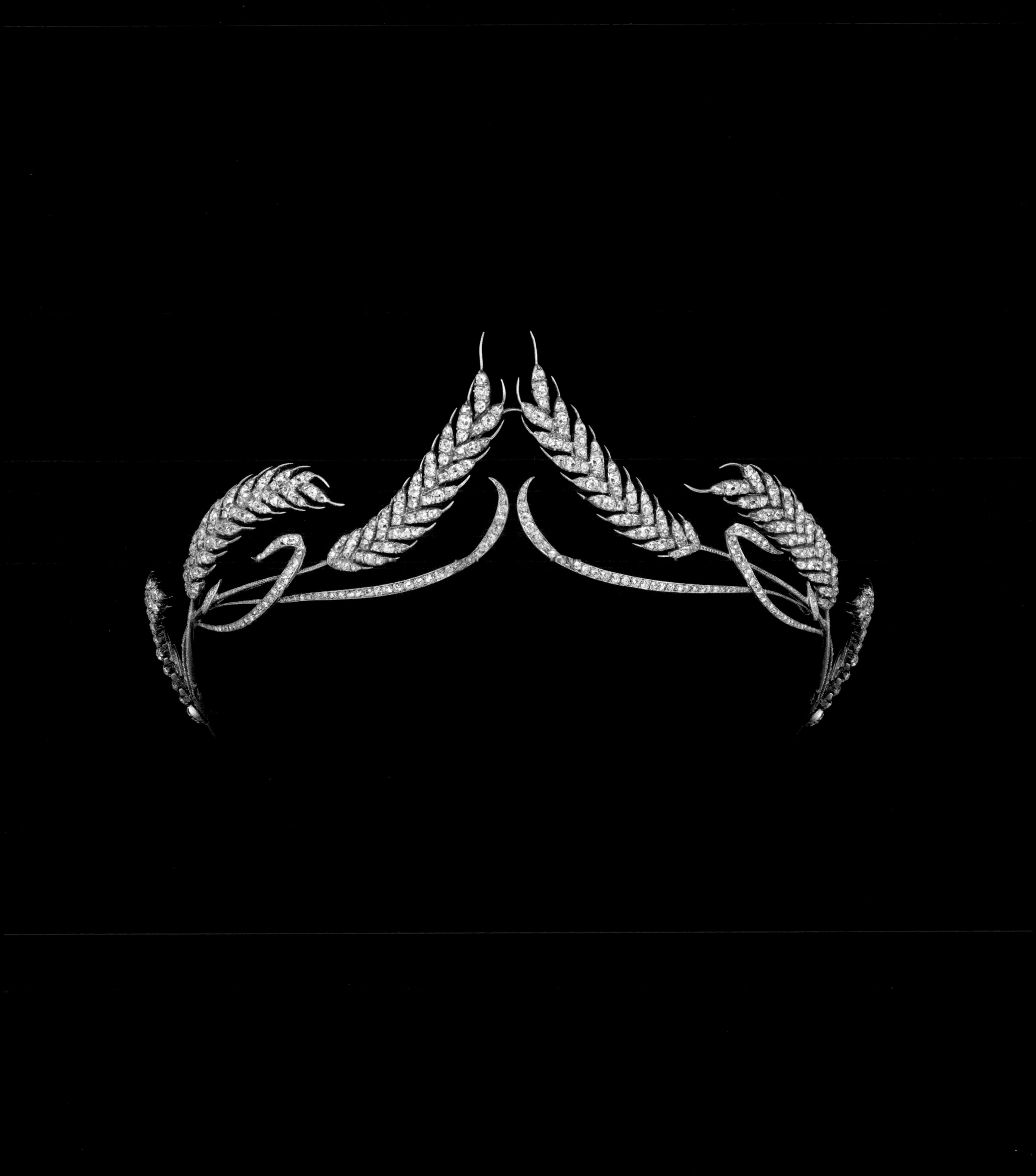

Monsieur Jean de Crèveco[eur]

120 rue de Longchamp

1910 Novem. 7.- Monté 1 Emeraude d'une applique remise en bague entourage brillants.

Employé:

1 Emeraude 5c 2/4 18 . 132 .

fourni:

22 diamants 2c 3/4 . 116 . . 1.

Une améthyste pour le centre d'une applique.

18.- Un diadème épis diamants formant devant de corsage à volonté

Employé:

10	diamants	1c . . 116/132 .
74	do	5c 3/4 18/116/132 .
33	do	3c 3/4 . 116/132 .
10	do	1c 3/4 18/116 . .

fourni:

85	diamants	3c 2/4 . . 132 .	
22	do	1c 3/4 . 116 . .	
28	do	. 2/4 . 116 . .	
10	d°	. 1/4 . . 132 .	
277	roses	1c . 18/116 . .	
20	do	. . 18 . . .	4.[illegible]

J B. Vente comptant 7 Juillet 1911 : 6000 f

Réduction : 50 f

Inv 3016. 1911 — 6.0[illegible]

1911 Juillet 7.- Récolté une épingle corail

Reporté f° 249. — 6.050. „ — 60[illegible]

1 Em.de 5c 3/4 18 . 132 .	9c 2775	. .
12 d° 2c 3/4 18 116 . .	mon	qim.mn
10 . . . 18 . . .	ate	ni.nc
Atelier 1306-607	12/11	rqn.ac
. 1070-627	16/11	u.te
Larcher	22/11	m .
.	7/1	o.ins
		rrog.gn
Ruthiot	10/11	ae .
1 st 2		
10 d° 1c . . 116/132 .	9c 2754	. .
74 N.R. 5c 3/4 18 116/132 .	.	. .
33 . 3c 3/4 . 116/132 .	.	. .
10 . 1c 3/4 18 116 . .	.	. .
3 épis non dém.tés	.	. .
Atelier 1130-952	30/12	rnen.en
2 st 6		
2 d° . . . 116/132 .	rue	ri.ie
10 N.R. . 3/4 18 . . .	rge	rro.ne
43 d° 2c . 18 . . .	oen	amn.te
40 . 1c 1/4 . 116 . .	ote	max.on
12 N.R. 1c . 18 116 . .	rae	itt.on
27 roses . 1/4	oee	ne .
120 . . 1/4 18 . . .	aan	itt.gn
50 . . 1/4	oee	ne .
30 . . . . . 132 .	gen	on.rn
50 . . 1/4 . . 132 .	orre	ie.me
16 d° . 1/4 . 116 . .	ooe	tg.in
10 N.R. . 1/4 . . 132 .	roe	mm.in
12 d° . 1/4	oee	ne .
20 roses . . 18 . . .	mme	ar.on
Larcher	31/12	ge .
Atelier 1380-970 mag.	7/1	mu.in
		m.ona,rn
Atelier 1736-1052	14/1	rom.rn
Larcher	21/1	am .
9t Atelier 89-17	1017	e.ue

FACING PAGE

59 *The "Crèvecœur" tiara commission*

Sales ledger November 18, 1910
Chaumet Archives, Paris

RIGHT

60 *The "Crèvecœur" tiara, transformed into a corsage ornament*

December 29, 1910
Gelatin silver-bromide glass negative no. 5126 and print
H. 18, W. 24 cm
Chaumet Archives, Paris

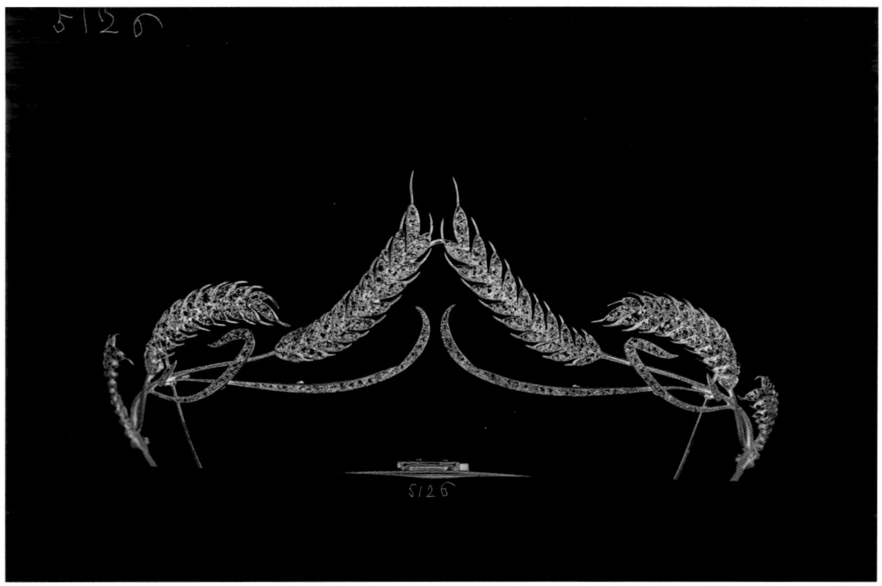

FACING PAGE AND PAGES 160–61

61 Leuchtenberg *tiara, transformable into a brooch and hair ornaments*

Jean-Baptiste Fossin (1786–1848)
Circa 1830–40
Gold, silver, emeralds, diamonds
H. 9, W. 14 cm
Chaumet Collection, Paris

The exceptional provenance of this tiara, once part of the collections of George, Duke of Leuchtenberg, grandson of Eugène de Beauharnais and great-grandson of Empress Joséphine, confirms its attribution to Nitot, in accordance with the family tradition. According to this same tradition, this tiara, transformable into a brooch, was the property of Queen Hortense, daughter of Joséphine and sister of Eugène. While it appears to have been acquired under the First Empire, the piece was probably modified between 1830 and 1840 by Fossin, Nitot's successor, to better correspond to the Romantic style, as reflected in its delicate floral design. As the Maison updated the art of head ornaments in this period, it drew endless inspiration from its precise and sensitive observation of the beauty of the plant world. The fashion was for ladies to wear fresh flowers in their hair and bodice, so jewelers captured in their designs the ephemeral beauty of small posies, garlands, and flowery sprigs, illuminated with magnificent stones, as in this naturalistic masterpiece set with 698 diamonds and 32 emeralds, including a large Colombian emerald of almost 13 carats. The *Leuchtenberg* tiara has two characteristics typical of Chaumet's designs: transformability and "*en trembleuse*" settings. Each of the eight elements making up the piece can be dismantled and worn as a head ornament, stomacher, or brooch, while the central flower, mounted on trembler springs, quivers lightly as the wearer moves, playing with the light to create the poetical illusion of a living thing. K. H.

MOINS CONNUE
MOINS TROUBLÉE

62 *Portrait of Queen Hortense*

Fleury François Richard (1777–1852)
1815

Oil on canvas
H 72.4, W. 51.3 cm
Dosne-Thiers Foundation,
Frédéric Masson Collection,
Institut de France, Paris

Hortense de Beauharnais, Joséphine's daughter from her first marriage to Alexandre, Viscount of Beauharnais, was in 1802 obliged to marry Napoleon's brother, Louis Bonaparte, King of Holland, in the hope that their children would be adopted by the emperor and inherit the imperial throne in the absence of an heir. Despite the birth of three children, including the future Napoleon III, the marriage was an unhappy one and the couple separated.

Hortense found in the arts a refuge from her unhappy relationship. In a letter dated 1809, her former tutor, Madame Campan, encouraged her to patronize the arts: "Purchase few jewels, but commission work from artists… the power of that class is immense, it can make a queen's reputation." Queen Hortense followed her advice and was generous toward artists, contributing through her acquisitions to the fashion for the "troubadour" style of painting. However, she purchased little jewelry, although she loved wearing it, like her mother. As did Joséphine, she commissioned numerous parures from Nitot & Fils, granted them her protection, and agreed to be a witness at the wedding of François-Regnault Nitot and Jeanne-Agathe Irisson in March 1809.

On the fall of the Empire in 1815, Hortense went into exile, and the personal jewels she took with her, which she sold as and when required, provided for her upkeep and her children's education. K.H.

BELOW

63 Keroüartz *necklace, transformable into a tiara*

1897

Gelatin silver-bromide glass negative
no. 1014 and print
H. 18, W. 24 cm
Chaumet Archives, Paris

FACING PAGE

64 Keroüartz *tiara, transformable into a necklace*

Joseph Chaumet (1852–1928)
1897

Gold, silver, diamonds, pearls
H. 7.1, W. 14.8 cm
Qatar Museums

In 1896, the royalist ladies of France set up a nationwide funding campaign for the wedding of Philippe, Duke of Orléans and Archduchess Maria Dorothea of Austria. Chaumet was commissioned to make a crown of brilliant-cut diamonds. The tiara designed by the jeweler was made up of inverted arches interspersed with laurel-leaf elements supporting large diamonds in tapered openwork mounts. This jewel could be converted into a necklace. It proved a popular design and was produced in slightly different versions. The marquis Frédéric de Keroüartz, belonging to one of the oldest families in Brittany, chose one for his fiancée, Louise d'Andigné, and gave it to her on the occasion of their wedding on August 10, 1897. According to documents in the Chaumet Archives, the jewel was delivered in its necklace form the day before the wedding. The intersections between the arches entwine stems that extend into a floating foliage motif, surmounted by fleuron from which hang large baroque pearls set in a cluster of brilliant-set filaments. A set of diamonds could originally replace the pearls that today adorn this transformable tiara/necklace, a magnificent example of Chaumet's craftsmanship and a seamless marriage of opulence and delicacy of design. C.V.

BELOW

65 *Navettes diamond necklace, transformable into a tiara*

Prints no. 24062
H. 24, W. 18 cm
Chaumet Archives, Paris

FACING PAGE AND PAGES 168–69

66 *Navettes diamond tiara, transformable into a neckclace*

Chaumet
1935
Platinum, diamonds
H. 5.4, W. 18.5 cm
Private collection

This impressive tiara was made in the mid-1930s, as the art deco style was beginning to wane yet still retained its expressive power. During this period Chaumet worked on the wedding basket of gifts for the Countess of Barcelona, and, later, that of Princess Alice of Bourbon-Parma, supplying jewelry pieces that still had a strong geometrical flavor. This tiara is composed of a series of oval elements linked together with arches and oriental-style intersections. These elements are all detachable, and can be attached to a ring and slipped onto a purpose-made chain of diamonds, transforming the ensemble into a magnificent necklace quite as majestic as the tiara itself. The ingenious design of these convertible jewels enabled them to be worn in very different ways, a versatility for which Chaumet would be renowned. C.V.

67 *Florets and foliage bandeau tiara, transformable into a bracelet*

Joseph Chaumet (1852–1928)
1909

Platinum, diamonds
L. 18, W. 1 cm
Chaumet Collection, Paris

This charmingly delicate and finely wrought small bandeau tiara transformable into a bracelet, sketches for which are still kept in the Maison's collection of drawings, is typical of the symbolic language used by the designers who worked with Joseph Chaumet. The composition of this small piece is a dual allusion to union and to womanhood: it alternates interlaced foliage motifs, suggesting links, with marguerite daisies representing Love, and whose Latin etymology (*margarita* means pearl) recalls that this flower has been associated with Venus since antiquity. It was delivered in June 1909 to Monsieur Dupré-La Tour, whose wedding was celebrated the following month, probably as a gift for his future wife. R.C.

68 *Study for the florets and foliage bandeau tiara*

Joseph Chaumet (1852–1928), drawing studio
1909
Graphite pencil, black ink, white gouache
Chaumet Collection, Paris

69 *Florets and foliage bandeau tiara, transformable into a bracelet*

June 28, 1909

Gelatin silver-bromide glass negative
no. 4422 and print
H. 13, W. 18 cm
Chaumet Archives, Paris

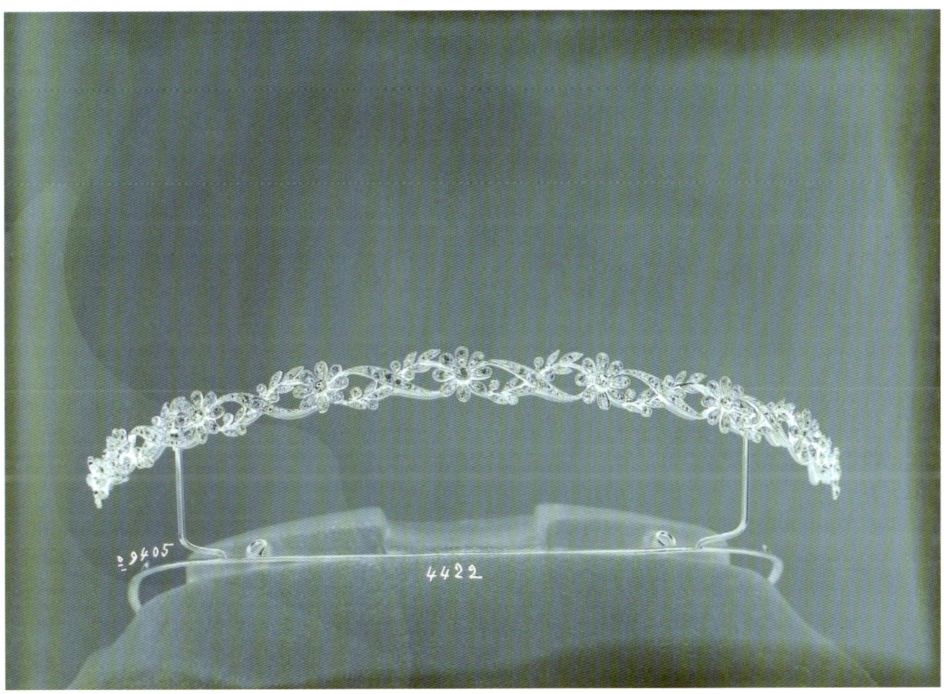

70 Promenades Impériales
transformable necklace

Les Mondes de Chaumet collection
Chaumet
2018
Gold, padparadscha sapphires, diamonds
Chaumet, Paris

Transformation has always been at the heart of Chaumet's designs. This necklace, centerpiece of the *Les Mondes de Chaumet* collection in 2018, is designed to be worn in different ways. It is a tribute to Russia, capturing the beauty of the Siberian winter. The orangey-pink hues of the padparadscha sapphires—a 16.31-carat pear, and a 9.03-carat cabochon—evoke the immensity of the dawn-lit snow-covered steppe, while the arrangement of diamonds is inspired by the intricate structures of ice crystals.

The *Promenades Impériales* necklace being assembled at the Chaumet jewelry workshop, 2018.

The head ornament offers the jeweler infinite creative possibilities. It enables the combination of themes, forms, and motifs, in a permanent dialogue with the arts of its times, drawing on the sources of inspiration dear to Chaumet. The tiara has its own poetic and metaphorical repertory, dominated by a fascination with the spectacle of nature. "Take these boughs, leaves, fruits, and flowers," wrote the poet Verlaine, and Chaumet would appropriate these verses to conjure up the magic of the ephemeral living world, the modest and wild flora and fauna beyond the cultivated garden. Venturing into fields and forests and to the banks of rivers and ponds, Chaumet transformed weeds into graceful plants, and captured flitting insects gathering pollen. Empress Joséphine's passion for the natural sciences and for botany in particular inspired her jeweler to come up with naturalistic themes, in a visionary, pre-Romantic spirit that resonated with the empress's sensibility. For her first appearance as Empress of the French, in July 1804, Joséphine chose the motif of wheat, symbol of prosperity and fertility. Another of the Maison's timeless classics is the laurel, allegory of victory and immortality. This naturalism evolved and blossomed throughout the Romantic era, when the fashion for wearing fresh flowers in the hair inspired jewelers to produce tiaras featuring foliage, branches, budding and flowering blooms, young and ripe fruit, and striking illusions of delicate bouquets, in a wealth of constantly reinvented symbolism.

The very essence of jewelry being to enhance the gems, the creation of an oscillation, a suspension, or an elevation in the design reveals the beauty of the stones and pearls and produces endless plays of light and subtle variations in their sparkle, in turn bestowing that miraculous aura upon the woman wearing them. This understanding of movement, an essential component in the most beautiful designs, to this day draws upon the observation of the natural world. A falling dew drop, leaves bending in the breeze, a spreading butterfly wing, the undulating lightness of a bird's feather: such is the grace and artistry of the jeweler Chaumet, whose poetic expression intensifies still in the universal symbolism of radiant suns and starry skies.

SYMBOLIC VARIATIONS

71 *Portrait of Princess Marie of Orléans*

Ary Scheffer (1795–1858)
1831

Oil on canvas
H. 97.5, W. 66.5 cm
Musée de la Vie Romantique, Paris

In the Romantic period, naturalism breathed new life into the art of jewelry. A fascination with botany, reminiscent of Empress Joséphine's passion for the subject, brought a profusion of natural and artificial flowers into the hairstyles and attire of fashionable ladies, enhanced with the sparkle of precious gemstones. Madame Junot d'Abrantès attributed the vogue to Princess Marie of Orléans, noting in one of her articles, published in 1840 in a famous fashion journal, *La Sylphide*: "She brought garlands into fashion, with a diamond and pearls in every flower."

Among King Louis-Philippe and Queen Marie-Amélie's ten children, Marie of Orléans was the most artistic. The princess showed a taste for artistic endeavor and a particular talent for sculpture, but her promising career was cut short by her premature death at the age of twenty-five. Ary Scheffer, who was one of her drawing tutors, painted her several times. This portrait conveys the modernity of Marie's melancholic sensibility, without any ornament other than that of the natural beauty of one of her famous garlands. These ephemeral creations, the most handsome of which were composed by the florist Batton, a neighbor of Fossin's, inspired jewelers to produce the most dazzlingly poetic and technically virtuosic head ornaments. From a simple diamond-set leaf pin that could be fixed into a spray of real flowers in the hair to a sumptuous tiara imitating bouquets and wreaths, the transient beauty of the plant world was heightened in its transformation into jewelry. K. H.

72 *Wild rose and jasmine tiara, known as the "Bedford" tiara*

Jean-Baptiste Fossin (1786–1848)
Circa 1830

Gold, silver, diamonds
H. 8.9, W. 20.3 cm
The Woburn Abbey Collection

This tiara in an entirely naturalistic style—acquired by Francis Russell, 7th Duke of Bedford, for his wife, Anna Maria Stanhope, daughter of the 3rd Earl of Harrington—is a lively depiction of wild nature. Flowers, fruit, and wild rose and jasmine leaves, treated entirely naturalistically, are composed to resemble a wreath of fresh flowers sprinkled with a diamond dew. The naturalistic illusion is heightened by tiny springs, allowing the flowers to quiver as the wearer moves.

Studies for the "Bedford" tiara in the Chaumet Archives display delicate, sensitive draftsmanship and accurate observation of details. In the wake of the diamond-studded floral bouquets that made his reputation, Fossin had a designer's talent that reinforced his mastery of the jeweler's art and enabled him to constantly invent new designs that were light and natural. Balzac admired this naturalness to the point of comparing Fossin—dubbed a "king" and a "powerhouse"—to Victor Hugo, then spearheading the style known as Romanticism, a truly poetic style in which everything was carefully arranged to "resemble reality just as Fossin's flowers of gems resemble the flowers in the fields." K.H.

Jean-Baptiste Fossin (1786–1848), drawing studio, preparatory drawing for the "Bedford" tiara, circa 1830. Graphite pencil. Chaumet Collection, Paris.

FACING PAGE AND PAGES 184–85

73 *Pansy flower tiara*

Jean-Baptiste Fossin (1786–1848)
Circa 1850

Silver, gold, diamonds
H. 7, W. 18 cm
Chaumet Collection, Paris

Among the tiaras in Chaumet's heritage collections, the pansy flower tiara is one of the most eloquent examples of the floral designs created under the man described by Honoré de Balzac as the "sublime Fossin," for the sophistication of his naturalistic designs. The Maison's designers worked from nature, as numerous documents in the archives show, and the execution of the flowers is strikingly realistic here. The unevenly attached petals, slight curve of their lobes, irregular design of the corolla, and the hollowed form of the flower, revealing the central diamond at its heart, perfectly reconstruct the anatomy of the field pansy. In the language of flowers, the pansy represents admiration of the loved one—the name of the flower coming from the French *pensée* (thought). Each flower could also be removed and worn as a brooch or hair ornament. R. C.

74 Passion Incarnat *lily tiara*

La Nature de Chaumet collection
Chaumet
2016

White and pink gold, red spinels, rhodolite garnets, green tourmalines, diamonds
H. 9, W. 14 cm
Chaumet Collection, Paris

The lily has been associated with the kings of France since Clovis in the fifth century, in accordance with the theological, legal, and historical theories developed under the ancien régime. It symbolizes divine purity, sovereignty, and strength, and is the indisputable emblem of royal power. This tiara, created in 2016 for the *La Nature de Chaumet* collection, while imbued with these fundamental notions, also expresses the natural beauty of this flower. The design here was inspired by the red Martagon lily, a full, luscious, and vigorous bloom, fascinating and feminine. It is evocative of Karl Joris Huysmans' description of its fragrance as "anything rather than chaste." "It is a mingling of honey and pepper," he wrote in *The Cathedral* (1898), in reference to its bewitching charm; one that conjures up both "the aphrodisiac conserves of the East and the erotic sweetmeats of the Indies." In keeping with the Maison's expertise in transformable jewels, the central flower can be removed and worn as a brooch. R.C.

FACING PAGE, TOP

75 *Pair of Mancini-style hair ornaments*

Attributed to Fossin & Fils
Circa 1840
Gold, silver, diamonds
H. 9.5, W. 5.6 cm
Chaumet Collection, Paris

This pair of hair ornaments in the Mancini-style, after Marie Mancini, niece of Cardinal Mazarin and first love of Louis XIV, was inspired by the fancy hair adornments favored by French aristocratic ladies in the mid-seventeenth century, who used them to embellish their ornate coiffures. The ornaments displayed here, reinterpretations from the Romantic era when hairdressers and *marchands de modes*, or fashion merchants, favored the use of fresh flowers, are inspired by the Virginia creeper. Featuring flexible diamond tassels, each carrying a magnificent irregular-cut Golconda diamond that captures the light in a lively manner, they were sure to add sparkle to the wearer's appearance. R.C.

FACING PAGE, BOTTOM

76 *Fuchsia brooch*

Attributed to Fossin
Circa 1840
Silver, gold, diamonds
H. 6.5, W. 5 cm
Private collection

Like the pansy flower tiara and the pair of Mancini-style hair ornaments, this small, remarkably finely wrought piece is another example of the sensitive and detailed observation of nature by the Maison's designers and jewelers. The piece manages to convey the soft bend of a fuchsia stem and the natural fall of the petals, revealing mobile stamens laden with briolette diamonds. In its interpretation of the fuchsia flower, with its red and purple hues evoking both amorous and mystical passions—a troubling ambivalence described by Marcel Proust in his description of the church in Combray in *Swann's Way*—this small brooch illustrates the power and subtlety of Chaumet's symbolic repertory of naturalistic forms. R.C.

BELOW

77 *Holly leaf brooch*

Joseph Chaumet (1852–1928)
Circa 1890
Gold, silver, fine pearls, diamonds
H. 9, W. 5 cm
Chaumet Collection, Paris

FACING PAGE

78 *Ivy leaf bracelet*

Jules Fossin (1808–1869)
1847
Gold, green enamel, diamonds, baroque natural pearls
H. 7, W. 7.8 cm
Chaumet Collection, Paris

PAGES 192–93

79 *Bunch of grapes parure*

Jean-Valentin Morel (1794–1860)
Circa 1850
Mauve pearls, emeralds, enamel, gold
Necklace L. 40 cm.
Bracelet H. 6.5, W. 6.5 cm.
Brooch H. 2.8, W. 4.1 cm
Chaumet Collection, Paris

In Romantic-era France during the Second Republic, jewelers had fully reappropriated crafts such as enameling and the art of chasing and began to produce designs that were not only formally inspired by nature but almost illusionistic in their naturalism. Jules Fossin's ivy leaf bracelet with its sinuous branches, symbolizing sentimental attachment, with leaves guilloched under green enamel and set with rows of diamonds tracing the veins, is a botanically realistic composition. Jean-Valentin Morel created designs in the same spirit as Jules Fossin, with whom he worked, as can be seen in the careful treatment of his bunch of grapes set. On a yellow gold mount (discreetly articulated for the necklace) made up of intertwined tendrils with chasing imitating the texture of the bark of a vine shoot, enameled or emerald-set vine leaves alternate in a natural manner with mauve-tinted pearls clustered in bunches, assembled invisibly with metal wire blackened like grape stems. In his *Scenes from a Courtesan's Life* (1838), Balzac gave a delicate description of the naturalism of "a complete set of ornaments ordered at Fossin's by an Englishwoman who went away without taking them" made of "bunches of jet grapes, of the finest workmanship…light as real vine-leaves," adding that "the artist had not forgotten the little graceful tendrils that clung among her curls, as the vine-tendrils cling to every branch." R.C.

80 *Bunch of grapes tiara and necklace parure*

Fossin & Fils
Circa 1825
Gold, turquoises
Necklace Diam. 18 cm. Tiara H. 5, W. 19 cm
Chaumet Collection, Paris

This day parure, made by Fossin in the 1820s, perfectly encapsulates the taste of the early Romantic period. Borrowing both from the vine, with its grapes in turquoises and finely chased gold leaves, and from the classical repertory with its stylized palmettes and Greek-key motifs and frieze, this ensemble combines the naturalistic inspiration for which the Maison became renowned and the classical-style ornaments of Nitot's designs several years earlier, under the First Empire. R.C.

FACING PAGE, TOP

81 *Fretwork and foliage bandeau tiara*

Joseph Chaumet (1852–1928)
1914

Platinum, diamonds
H. 2.5, W. 17 cm
Private collection

Another example of this subtle balance between plant-inspired forms and the ornamental repertoire of architecture, this bandeau tiara commissioned by the Marquis of Labriffe in 1914 features a particularly harmonious combination of curving lines and right-angled elements. The key pattern gives the design its powerful and perfectly symmetrical structure, while a delicate undulating foliage motif animates the composition. When removed from the discreet frame that turns it into a bandeau, thanks to hinges in its structure, this piece can be worn as a choker. R. C.

FACING PAGE, BOTTOM

82 *Fretwork tiara*

Joseph Chaumet (1852–1928)
Circa 1910

Millegrain platinum, diamonds
H. 2.8, W. 16.6 cm
Qatar Museums

The key pattern or fret, deriving from the decorative vocabulary of ancient architecture, was a popular motif under the Empire and made its way into jewelry. Joséphine owned a fretwork tiara in 1804, and Pauline Borghese owned a bandeau with alternating frets and cameos. A century later, the theme came back into fashion and Chaumet produced its first fretwork tiara in 1904. Versions of the key pattern followed in the years that followed, a notable example being a tiara acquired in 1925 by Viscountess Marie-Laure de Noailles, an illustrious figure of the art world and loyal client of the house. Some of these fretwork designs featured a central ornament topped with a diamond or colored stone finial. C. V.

83 Vertiges *tiara*

Scott Armstrong for Chaumet
2017

White gold, rose gold, diamond, citrines, yellow garnets, green beryls, green tourmalines, emeralds
H. 10.7, W. 16.3 cm
Chaumet Collection, Paris

On the occasion of the exhibition *Imperial Splendours: The Art of Jewellery Since the 18th Century* held in 2017 in Beijing's Forbidden City, Chaumet gave carte blanche to students at Central Saint Martins in London to create a tiara for the twenty-first century. The winner of the competition was Scott Armstrong, now a designer at the Chaumet studio. He drew inspiration from the Maison's naturalistic tradition and also from the book *The French Formal Garden* (1974), in his interpretation of an aesthetic from the seventeenth-century landscape design of André Le Nôtre, master gardener of Louis XIV. The tiara's juxtaposition of free lines and curves suggests an architecture in which details break with the overall symmetry. The composition of tourmalines and garnets creates a succession of green and yellow hues to astonishing effect. The majestic classicism of formal gardens and the surprising design features are combined with a light, elevated style that is characteristic of the Maison. The art of composition and reinterpretation of conventional codes perfectly corresponds to the Chaumet landscape.

84 *Portrait of Empress Joséphine*

Jean-Baptiste Regnault (1754–1829)
Circa 1809
Oil on canvas
H. 59.4, W. 46.8 cm
Dosne-Thiers Foundation,
Institut de France, Paris

With the neoclassical movement, the laurel became a popular motif in head ornaments in the early nineteenth century. Like victorious warriors in Greek and Roman times, Napoleon chose it for his imperial crown as a symbol of his power, while Joséphine also adopted it to display her sovereign status, wearing a laurel-leaf tiara for the coronation. Nitot appropriated the classical symbol in turn, creating harmoniously symmetrical arrangements that were characteristic of the imperial jewels. The tiara was the centerpiece of the sumptuous ceremonial parures supplied by the jeweler, the crown that drew the eye, focused and raised people's gazes, and transfigured and deified the wearer. In this parure, depicted with precision by Regnault, the empress's tiara features two large laurel branches studded with diamonds that joined above the forehead, over a floral band set with splendid emeralds, a type of naturalistic composition typical of the Empire style. K. H.

FACING PAGE AND PAGES 204–5

85 Firmament Apollinien *Laurel tiara*

La Nature de Chaumet collection
Chaumet
2016
Gold, silver, sapphires
Chaumet Paris

For over two hundred years, since the first tiaras supplied to Empress Joséphine, Chaumet has continued to reinterpret the laurel motif, a classic among classics in the jeweler's ornamental repertoire. The *Firmament Apollinien* tiara, designed in 2016, adopts the stylistic codes of the Maison, in harmony with contemporary tastes. While following the same principle of symmetrical composition as its illustrious neoclassical predecessors, *Firmament Apollinien* has a freer naturalism, referencing the Greek myth of the nymph Daphne turned into a laurel tree to escape the god's passionate advances. As Apollo's sacred tree, its evergreen leaves a symbol of immortality, the laurel remains the timeless allegory of victory, and here celebrates the beauty and character of an unconquered woman.

This exceptional bejeweled head ornament, set with a central 14.55-carat Ceylon sapphire, diamonds, and a row of cabochon sapphires, can be transformed into a simpler bandeau tiara, by detaching the upper part affixed with a discreet system of clips. K.H.

CHAUMET

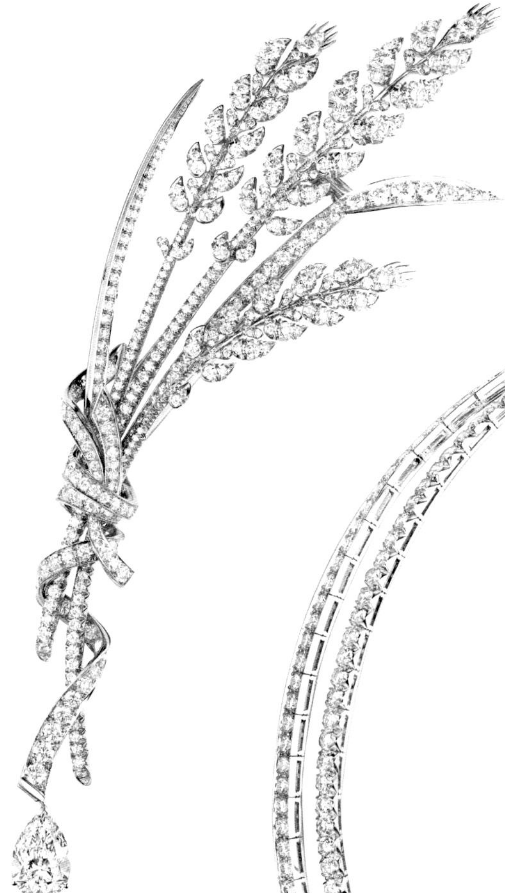

FACING PAGE

86 Offrandes d'Été *parure: wheat-ear tiara, necklace, brooch, ring*

La Nature de Chaumet collection
Chaumet
2016
White gold, diamonds
Necklace Diam. 42 cm
Chaumet Paris
Private collection

RIGHT

87 *Portrait of Empress Joséphine wearing a wheat-ear tiara*

Jean-Baptiste-Jacques Augustin (1759–1832)
Early nineteenth century
Gouache, watercolor, signed left Augustin
H. 6.7, W. 5.4 cm
Frame with metal stand H. 9, W. 7.5 cm
Fondation Napoléon, Paris

The attribute of Ceres, Roman goddess of the harvest, and symbol of prosperity and fertility, the ear of wheat was a popular motif in First Empire jewelry and a favorite of Empress Joséphine. Nitot produced many variations of the theme, which continued to be fashionable in the Belle Époque and still inspires designs today. This contemporary parure celebrates summertime, the earth's bountiful riches, and the return to a nurturing life, and draws on the Maison's earliest sources of creativity in a new naturalistic interpretation. The freshly cut sheaves, plump with ripe grains in diamonds, are tied together with a piece of twine from which a pear-shaped diamond is suspended. K. H.

88 *Reed brooch*

Joseph Chaumet (1852–1928)
Circa 1893
Gold, diamonds
H. 28, W. 19 cm
Private collection of H.R.H.
Princess of Hanover

Borrowed from silver tableware, the reed motif met with great favor in the Belle Époque. The reed's long, slender leaves and straight stem with flowers that form either a plume or a furry, cylindrical spike offer fine graphic possibilities. In the late nineteenth century, it was one of the Chaumet designers' preferred realistic plant motifs. The exceptional size of this brooch and the quality of its composition make it a masterpiece of turn-of-the-century naturalism. The plant's free movement in space and beautifully observed bent leaves are constrained only by a small piece of knotted twine, turning them into a sheaf.

One of the reasons for the enduring popularity of the reed motif during this period is that it is a powerful symbol in French classical culture. In Jean de La Fontaine's famous fable *The Oak and the Reed* (1668), the weak reed bends but never breaks, while the powerful oak is blown down by the storm. The great seventeenth-century philosopher Blaise Pascal associated it with the human condition, writing in his *Pensées* (1670), "Man is but a reed, the most feeble thing in nature; but he is a thinking reed… But, if the universe were to crush him, man would still be more noble than that which killed him, because he knows that he dies and the advantage which the universe has over him; the universe knows nothing of this." K. H.

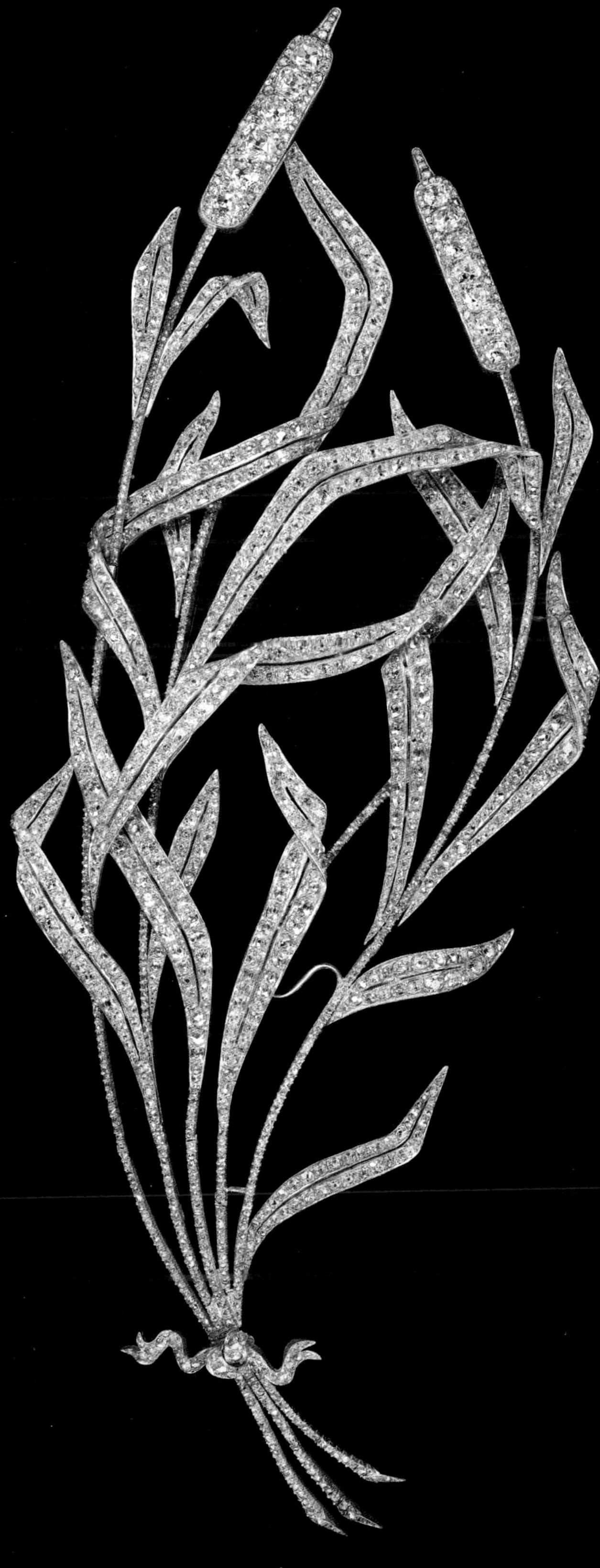

PAGES 210–11

89 *Sunburst aigrette*

Joseph Chaumet (1852–1928)
1916

Gold, platinum, emerald, diamonds
H. 5.5, W. 13 cm
Chaumet Collection, Paris

BELOW

90 *Star brooch*

Joseph Chaumet (1852–1928)
Circa 1900

Gold, silver, diamonds, emerald
Private collection

FACING PAGE

91 *Crescent moon brooch, transformable into an aigrette*

Joseph Chaumet (1852–1928)
Circa 1890

Gold, silver, pearls
H. 4.2, W. 4 cm (without the feather)
Chaumet Collection, Paris

Since ancient times, the stars, richly symbolic for all humanity, have been a constant source of inspiration for jewelry designers. As reflected in the Chaumet Archives, sun, moon, and star motifs, in brooches and tiaras, met with considerable success from the late Belle Époque to the Roaring Twenties.

This spectacular aigrette (pages 210–11) perfectly illustrates the taste for these celestial inspirations at the turn of the last century. It takes the form of a large sun whose powerful rays radiate from a central emerald with a lush *jardin* (or "garden," a term for the inclusions present in the gem) haloed with two rows of diamonds. In addition to the polylobate design of the central section, and the millegrain work on the visible side of the "knife-edge" wires structuring the motif, the false symmetry of the intermediary rays gives this accessory a real sense of kinetic energy. R.C.

92 *Wings tiara belonging to Mrs. Payne Whitney (née Gertrude Vanderbilt)*

Joseph Chaumet (1852–1928)
1910

Platinum, diamonds, enamel
Left: H. 4.7, W. 15 cm. Right: H. 4.7, W. 16 cm
Chaumet Collection, Paris

Jewelry with designs inspired by birds' wings were in vogue until after World War II, as shown by numerous examples that have come down to us. Wings tiaras, designed for women of character, were inspired by the winged helmets worn by the Valkyries of Wagner's operas, figures of Norse mythology. The wings could be repositioned as desired, and either worn on a frame on the top of the head or as brooches, individually or as a pair.

Among the most spectacular was the pair belonging to one of the most influential American figures of the early twentieth century, Mrs. Payne Whitney, née Gertrude Vanderbilt. Today it dazzles among the showpieces in Chaumet's

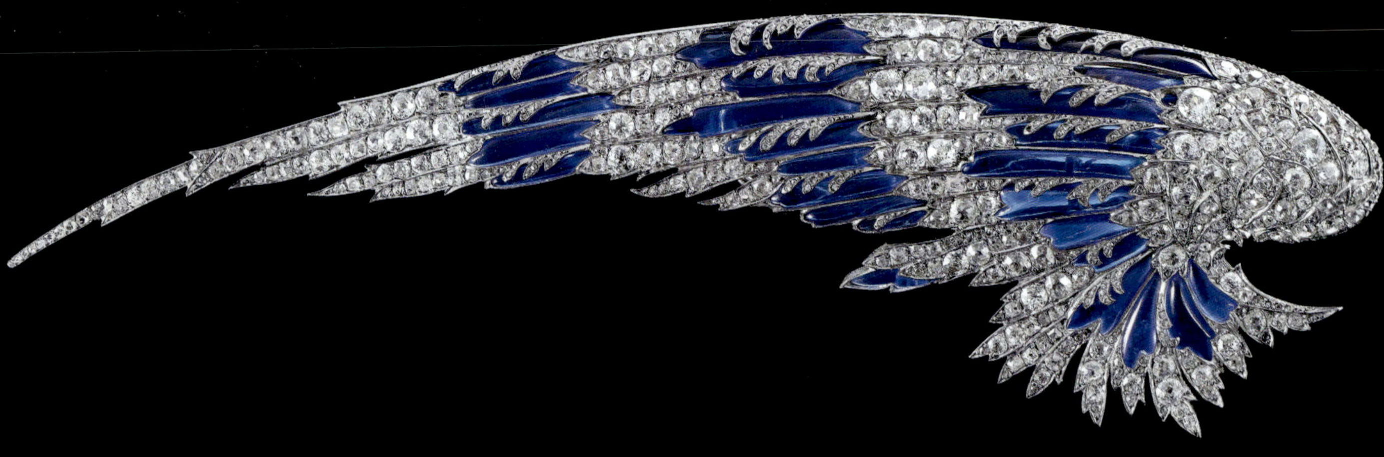

collection of historic jewels. Acquired in New York on July 6, 1910, set with 566 diamonds and 708 rose-cut diamonds, the wings are worn as a tiara mounted on a frame.

In marrying Harry Payne Whitney in 1896, Vanderbilt added her family's immense fortune to that of the Standard Oil firm, offering the couple almost unlimited financial means. Passionate about jewels, a great patron, and the founder of the Whitney Museum of American Art, she was among Chaumet's clientele of American billionaires in the Belle Époque. K. H.

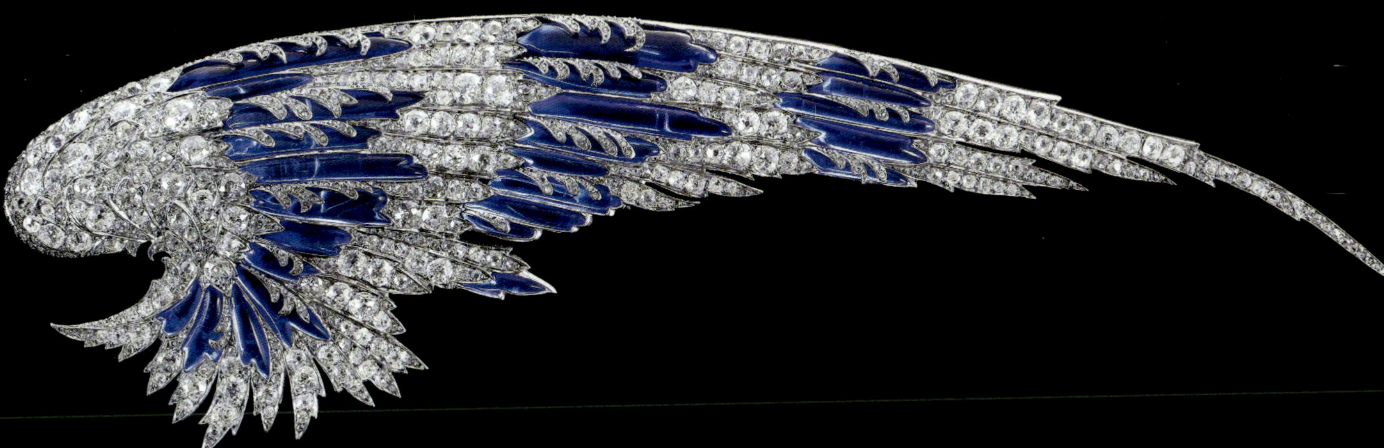

93 *Peacock feather brooch, transformable into a sapphire brooch*

Prosper Morel (1825–1908)
Circa 1870
Gold, silver, sapphires, rubies, diamonds
H. 14, W. 4.5 cm
Faerber Collection

This peacock feather with its large sapphire for an eyespot is a perfect example of the transformable jewel, one of Chaumet's signature specialties. The 32-carat stone, mounted *"en trembleuse"*—on tremblers, i.e. tiny springs—can be detached and worn as a brooch. The Maison has always prioritized the quality and beauty of its stones, seeking to show them off to their best advantage. The peacock feather, that quintessential symbol of display, was very popular in the second half of the nineteenth century, and was interpreted by various jewelers, including Prosper Morel, who worked in the naturalistic vein introduced by Fossin. The barbs of the vane, meticulously set with diamonds, branch off the central rachis that is partially set with rubies in gold. C.V.

94 *Wing brooch belonging to the Princess of Ligne*

Joseph Chaumet (1852–1928)
Circa 1907

Gold, silver, rubies, diamonds
H. 3.5, W. 10.5 cm
Chaumet Collection, Paris

This extremely elegant wing, once part of a pair, was purchased by the Princess of Ligne circa 1907. It could be worn as a head ornament opposite its twin, or detached to be worn as a brooch or to adorn a corsage. Some wings were mostly set with diamonds, while others had blue or ruby enamel decoration, like this one. The illustrious house of Ligne—related by marriage to the La Rochefoucauld and Cossé-Brissac families, already clients of Chaumet—appears regularly in the Maison's books. C.V.

95 *Hummingbird aigrette*

Joseph Chaumet (1852–1928)
Circa 1880

Gold, silver, rubies, diamonds
H. 10, W. 5 cm
Chaumet Collection, Paris

96 *Pair of hummingbird aigrettes, transformable into brooches*

Joseph Chaumet (1852–1928)
Circa 1890
Gold, silver, rubies, diamonds, demantoid garnets
H. 4, W. 4 cm
Chaumet Collection, Paris

BELOW

97 *Series of preparatory studies for the* Piaf *brooch*

Béatrice de Plinval for Chaumet
1967–1968
Graphite, watercolor, gouache
Chaumet Collection, Paris

FACING PAGE

98 Piaf *brooch*

Béatrice de Plinval for Chaumet
1968
Gold, diamond, lapis lazuli, coral
The Prince's Palace Collections, Monaco

Béatrice de Plinval's very first designs for Chaumet betrayed her keen interest in ornithology, providing a naturalistic glimpse of little birds on a branch. While her sketches wittily stressed their cute roundness, the jewelry workshop brought out the comic poetry of a sparrow (*piaf* in French) with ruffled feathers, perched on a branch of coral. The naturalism is underscored by the use of *or sauvage* (gold with a "natural" finish).

Made for stock, this imaginative item was bought by Major Paul-Louis Weiller, a pioneering pilot and later aviation magnate as well as a collector and patron, who presented it to H.S.H. Princess Grace of Monaco in 1968. K.H.

FACING PAGE

99 *Butterfly brooch*

Attributed to
Joseph Chaumet (1852–1928)
Circa 1895
Gold, silver, rubies, diamonds
H. 6.3, W. 6.6 cm
Private collection

RIGHT

100 *Wild rose and butterfly corsage ornament*

Joseph Chaumet (1852–1928)
Circa 1895
Gold, silver, rubies, diamonds
H. 15, W. 9 cm
Private collection

While flowers and plants continued to be sketched from life by the Maison's designers, before being faithfully reproduced by the jewelers—as illustrated in this particularly realistic rendering of a branch of wild rose with silver contours tracing the stems, leaves, and fruit—the animal kingdom, and particularly insects, remained a rich source of inspiration. This is reflected in the drawings collection, where the butterfly is undoubtedly the most common motif, besides a surprising diversity of creatures ranging from shield bug to may bug and from grasshopper to dragonfly. The butterfly, suggestive of lightness and femininity, has been a symbol of the soul and reincarnation since ancient times and is associated with Psyche and dreams. It was a popular motif at the turn of the twentieth of century, particularly for brooches. The butterflies here, both of them mounted on "*en trembleuse*" settings, would come to life at the slightest movement of the wearer, elegantly quivering on the trembler springs to which they are attached. The rubies in the second brooch have a remarkably deep, dark red hue, recalling the particular focus placed on the stones under Joseph Chaumet. R.C.

101 *Wild rose tiara*

Joseph Chaumet (1852-1928)
Circa 1922
Platinum, diamonds, pearls
H. 8, W. 16 cm
Private collection

A masterpiece of lightness, the wild rose tiara was made at a time when the decorative conventions of art deco were already in wide use. Yet its motifs are not stylized and offer a late example of naturalism, one of the great specialties of the Maison. Botanists will observe the accuracy of the design, with the open sepals arising from the hypanthium, revealing the natural pearls that represent closed flower buds. While the rosebush signifies a poetic tribute, the flower symbolizes poetry and passion. The wild rose is also associated with secrecy, for its five slightly cupped petals hide its most intimate part. This is probably why the wild rose motif appears in confessionals and private state rooms: "Ce qui est dit sous la rose ne doit pas être révélé, vérité ou mensonge, l'églantine garde le secret" (What is said under the rose must not be revealed, truth or lie, the wild rose keeps her secret). C.V.

102 *Octopus necklace*

Robert Lemoine (1909–1976)
for Chaumet
1970

Frosted rock crystal, curved jasper, diamonds, rubellite
L. 24, W. 12 cm
Private collection

Through the centuries, Chaumet has made collar, sautoir, and pendant necklaces in every shape and form. From the dazzling neoclassical necklaces worn by Empress Joséphine to the long sautoirs of the Roaring Twenties worn by women enjoying their new freedom and movement, the quintessence of the Maison's creative work is to be found in this centerpiece of the art of jewelry.

Made by the sculptor Robert Lemoine, this surprising necklace features a rock-crystal octopus clinging to a garland of carved-jasper seaweed and clutching a trapped rubellite in its diamond-studded tentacles. The necklace was part of the wedding basket of gifts commissioned by Sir Valentine Abdy, 6th Baronet of Albyns, for his future wife, Mathilde de La Ferté. It reflects a renewed interest, after 1968, in the iconic works of the surrealist artists of the 1930s, such as Salvador Dalí, Man Ray, and Meret Oppenheim, and symbolizes the power of a passionate relationship verging on possessive attachment. K. H.

103 Shell *corsage ornament*

Joseph Chaumet (1852–1928)
1913
Gold, silver, diamond, 322-carat aquamarine
H. 10, W. 8.5, D. 2.3 cm
Private collection

This corsage ornament—an item of jewelry pinned to the bodice of an evening gown—features an impressive 322-carat aquamarine. Among its many virtues, aquamarine is said to guarantee newlyweds a happy marriage and mutual faithfulness. And indeed, this brooch was a wedding gift.

Here Chaumet's artistry has created a setting for this magnificent stone that evokes the sea, which is a semantic play on the name of the stone itself ("aquamarine" meaning "sea water"). The large blue stone is surrounded by diamonds suggesting shells, water droplets, and icicles, all made mobile by many tiny hinges in the setting. R. C./K. H.

Design for the *Shell* corsage ornament, 1913.
Graphite pencil, gouache, ink wash.
Chaumet Collection, Paris.

The unique radiance that a tiara lends to a woman's beauty, its power of statement, and even transfiguration, have made it a fashion accessory that is without equivalent. It has accompanied the evolution of female attire through time, conveying an art of living as well as the elegance of the wearer and her social status. It has seen multiple exercises in style, worn as a crown to express sovereignty, or as a bandeau across the forehead in the Roaring Twenties. From the feathered aigrettes of the Belle Époque to the less ostentatious and easier-to-wear designs of today, the head ornament is synonymous with an art of seduction that begins in the privacy of mirrored boudoirs. It requires special preparation, and is set off by the hair that supports it and by the manner in which it is worn. Jewelry is a kinetic art: an immobile beauty when admired in the jeweler's showcase, it takes on its full dimension, like all the decorative arts relating to human adornment, with the movement of the wearer. This sensorial and sensual experience is the unspoken complement to the immediate visual delight it elicits.

The tiara has today broken free from its image as an attribute of power or of the sacred dimension of the wedding ceremony, to emerge as a symbol of feminine beauty in all its glory. As an enduring part of festive and ceremonial finery, updated in contemporary designs that shake off the weight of history, it encapsulates the magic of a moment, the passing from the shadows into the light, when it is set on a woman's head to transform her for her presentation to the world. With the thrill of her revelation and appearance comes the magical radiance in which a tiara haloes any woman, heightening her aura. Since 1780, Chaumet has turned this into an art.

MAKING AN ENTRANCE

104 *"Bessborough" tiara*

Marcel Chaumet (1886–1964)
1931
Platinum, diamonds
H. 5, W. 16 cm
Private collection

On his appointment as Governor General of Canada in 1931, the 9th Earl of Bessborough received from his colleagues at De Beers, where he had acted as deputy chairman, the gift of a 12-carat navette- or marquise-cut diamond. He had it mounted in a tiara in a beautifully symmetrical composition with the strong, clean lines characteristic of the art deco style. His wife, Roberte de Neuflize Ponsonby, a Frenchwoman whose wedding basket of gifts had also been made by Chaumet ten years previously, wore it to perfection.

In 1937, when Joseph Kennedy was presented to the Court of St. James's as United States Ambassador, his wife Rose Elizabeth Fitzgerald Kennedy donned the same piece. Although it was customary for married woman to wear a diamond tiara to such an occasion, she did not own one. "It had simply never occurred to me before coming to England that I would ever need one. My new and sympathetic friend Lady Bessborough lent me hers, and it proved to be most flattering and magnificent. It fitted well...," she recounted in her memoirs, *Times to Remember* (1974). Some forty years later, she remembered the emotions stirred by such an event: "The great night arrived. I had already been to the hairdresser that afternoon and my hair was done in a way to receive Lady Bessborough's tiara.... The man from Molyneux came over to check details and to pin and to secure our three head feathers at the proper angle, as I had no idea about how this should be done. A hairdresser was there to place the tiara on my carefully constructed coiffure.... I went into my husband's room to show him my elegance.... The girls meanwhile had been having their own special attentions and in a few minutes, fully as excited or more so than I, came running in to see us and be seen. More exclamations all round. Then downstairs to be viewed by the younger children who were duly impressed." K. H.

Yousuf Karsh (1908–2002), *Roberte de Neuflize Ponsonby, Countess of Bessborough*, wearing her Chaumet tiara, 1931.

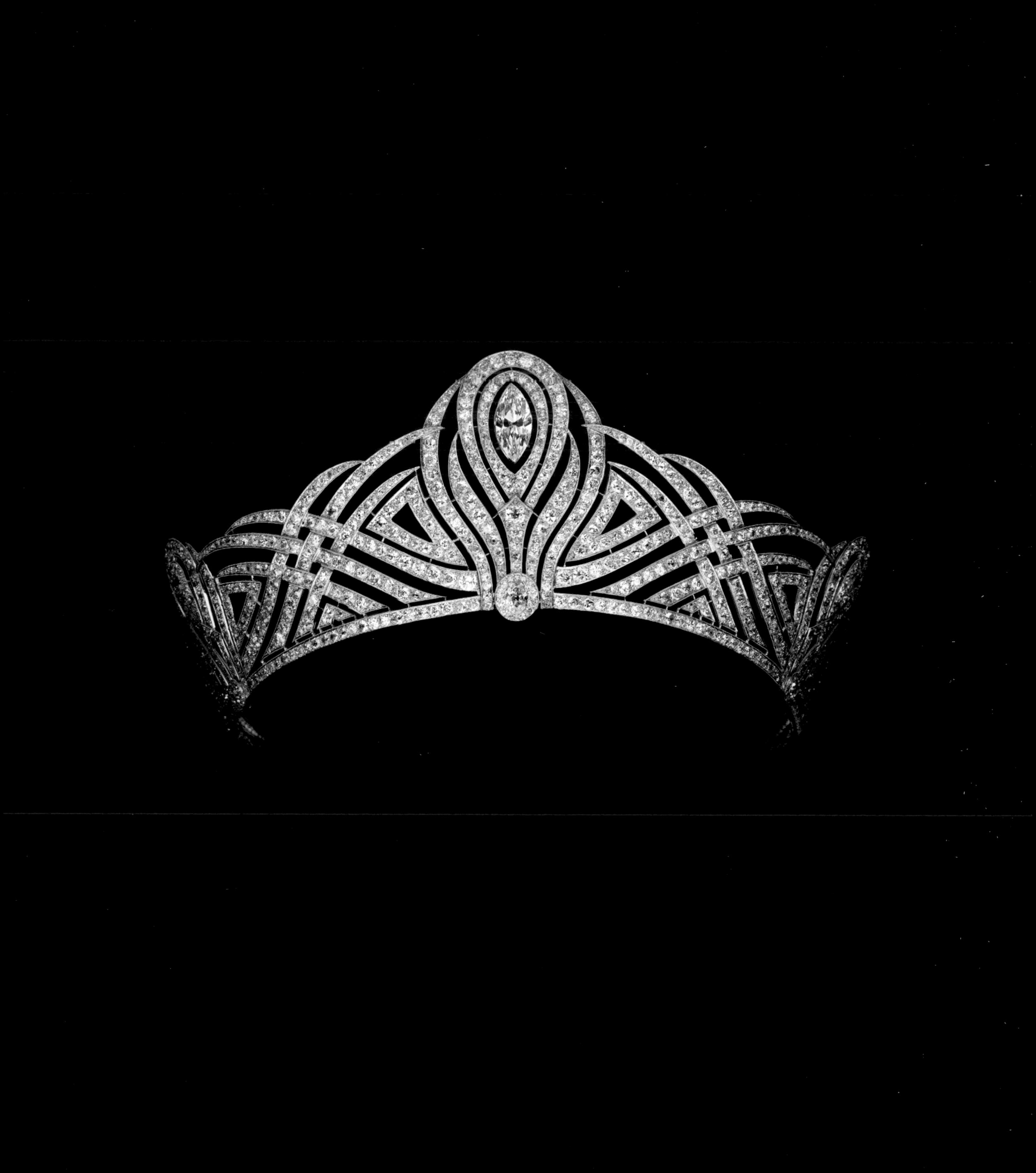

105 *Tiara, transformable into a corsage ornament, belonging to Marquise Maeda*

Two prints from gelatin silver-bromide glass negatives nos. 7862 and 7965, dated July 26, 1920
H. 30, W. 40 cm and H. 18, W. 24 cm
Chaumet Archives, Paris

Kikuko Maeda, second wife of Marquis Toshinari Maeda, military attaché to Great Britain at the Japanese Embassy in London, poses in her formal attire, worn for a presentation to the Court of St. James's at Buckingham Palace in 1929. The tiara she wears, along with the feathers required by the dress code for this ceremony, had been purchased from Chaumet in 1920 by Maeda's first wife, Namiko. Typical of the Japanese clientele from diplomatic circles in the immediate postwar period, Namiko Maeda ordered many items of jewelry from Chaumet from 1920 until her death in 1923.

The Chaumet Archives carry a record of this commission, delivered on May 24, 1920: "a diamond tiara with center detachable to be worn as a corsage ornament." With its geometric foliage characteristic of art deco, this tiara was a flexible bandeau circling the head, adapted to suit a short, slightly wavy hairstyle, and drawing attention to the facial features. The central motif is detachable and can be transformed into a corset ornament with the addition of a bow pendant. K.H.

Marquise Maeda wearing the Chaumet tiara transformable into a corsage ornament, 1929.

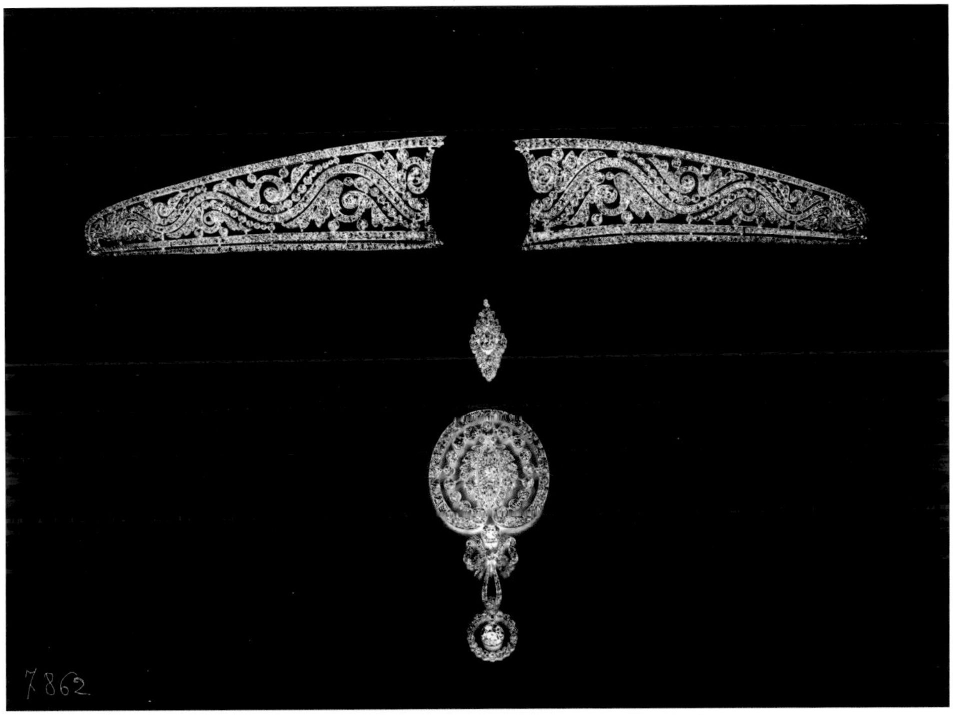
7862

2965

PAGES 240–41

106 *Sun tiara belonging to Princess Yusupov*

Joseph Chaumet (1852–1928)
1913–14

Print from gelatin silver-bromide glass no. 6467, dated July 26, 1920
H. 24, W. 30 cm
Chaumet Archives, Paris

FACING PAGE Princess Yusupov wearing the sun tiara made by Chaumet, 1914.

Chaumet's most significant orders from Russia were for the niece of Czar Nicholas II, Irina Alexandrovna Romanov. Considered one of the most beautiful princesses in Europe, in 1914 she married the handsome prince Felix Yusupov, who would become notorious for helping to plot the assassination of Rasputin in 1916. In view of the wedding, Felix's mother, Princess Zinaida Yusupova, whose fortune surpassed even that of the czar, deposited family stones and jewels with Chaumet to have them made into the most lavish wedding basket of gifts of the time. In his memoirs, *Lost Splendor: The Amazing Memoirs of the Man Who Killed Rasputin* (1954), Felix Yusupov wrote: "When we passed through Paris, old Chaumet brought us Irina's jewels, which he had reset during our absence [on their honeymoon in Egypt]. He had not wasted his time: the five sets he had designed in diamonds, pearls, rubies, emeralds and sapphires seemed each more beautiful than the other. They were much admired in London." When the Bolshevik Revolution broke out in 1917, Felix and Irina were forced into exile and hid many of their jewels in a wall of their palace in Moscow. In 1925, Princess Irina's jewels were discovered in the palace, which now housed the Military History Museum, by an employee of the institution, and were examined by specialists and redistributed by order of the Soviet government.

Among this exceptional collection was a triple-sun articulated diamond tiara, all trace of which has been lost, as is the case of other parures from 1914. In the photo from the Chaumet Archives, the setting for the central stone is still empty. Its size and shape suggests it was to receive the famous Polar Star, a 40-carat diamond from the Yusupov collection. The sun motif, symbol of Louis XIV's reign in the seventeenth century, was very fashionable in the years preceding World War I. It was not new among Chaumet's repertory of styles, but here the jeweler gave the design a modern feel that heralded the strong lines of art deco. The bold articulated structure enabled it to be placed very close to the forehead, giving the illusion of a radiant halo of light illuminating the woman wearing it. K. H.

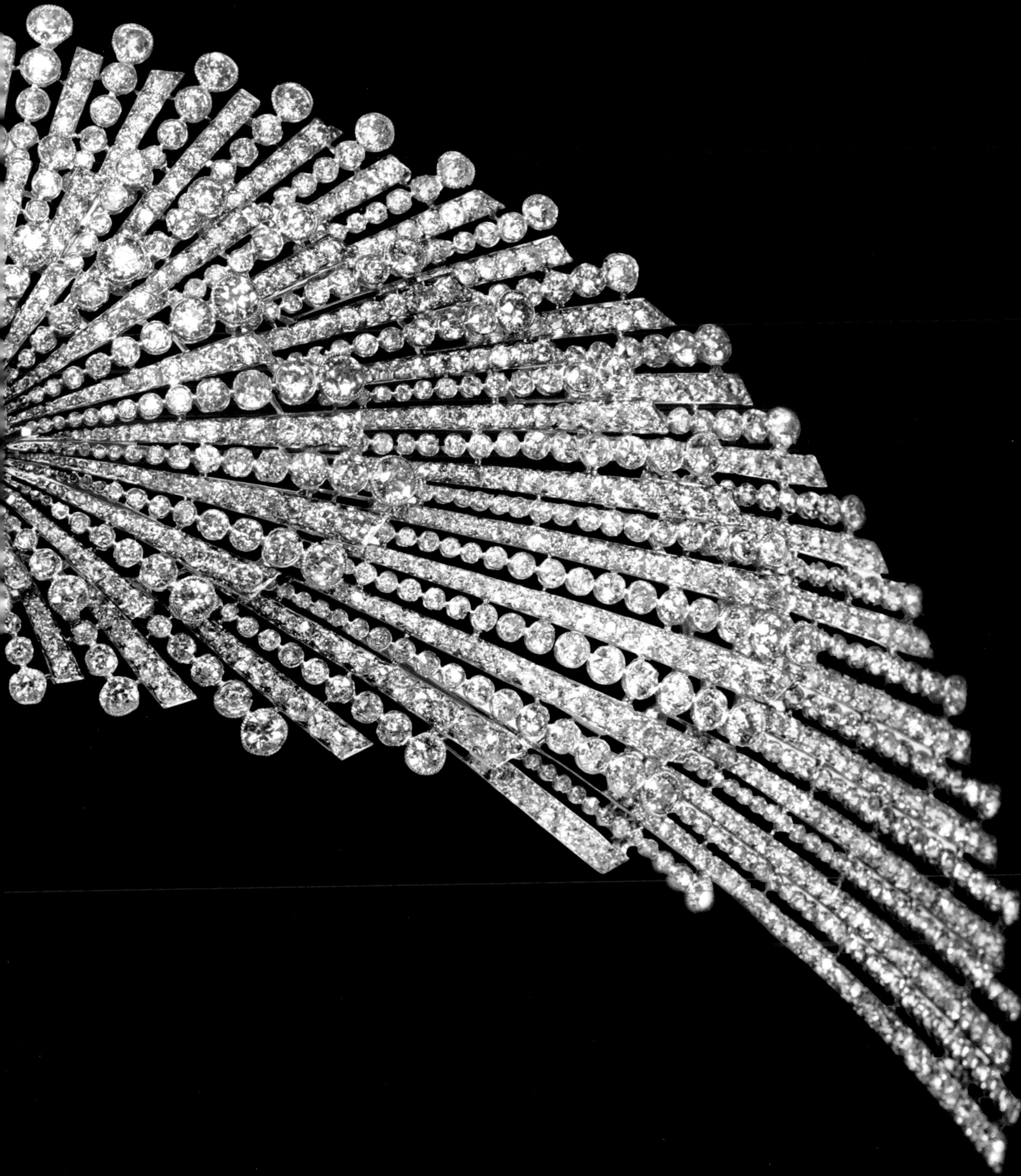

CHAUMET
Place VENDOME
N.12

107 *Chaumet Place Vendôme No. 12, sketch for a Chaumet advertisement: tiaras and bandeaux worn "à la Joséphine"*

Circa 1920

Charcoal, gouache, India ink
H. 77, W. 55.5 cm
Chaumet Collection, Paris

During the Roaring Twenties, women's bodies were liberated and clothing fashions reshaped the female silhouette. Dresses with dropped waists were all the rage, and short hair, either curly or straight in the style of Louise Brooks, film star and muse of the day, became fashionable. Jewelry followed suit: tiaras came down lower on the forehead; earrings lengthened, as did necklaces, which became sautoirs. A motif emerged in the early 1910s—named the *écu compté* by the workshops—in the form of overlapping discs: a succession of semi-circular elements radiating out from the center. Among the numerous versions produced was a tiara made for the wedding basket of gifts for Princess Irina Yusupov of Russia in 1914, and another purchased a year earlier by the Duchess of Medinaceli. C.V.

Joseph Chaumet (1852–1928), drawing studio, study for a tiara with the *écu compté* or overlapping disc motif, circa 1920. Gouache, ink wash, and gouache highlights. Chaumet Collection, Paris.

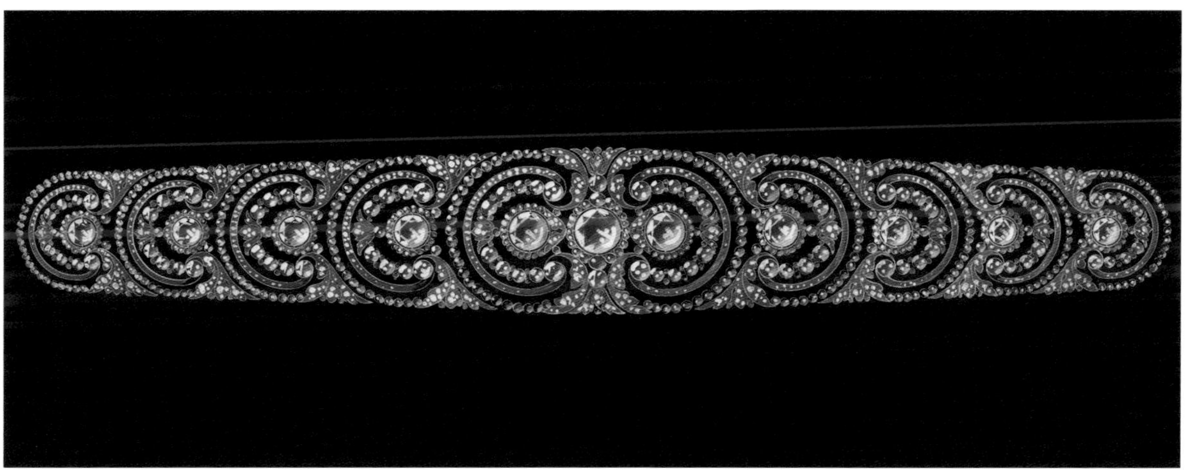

BELOW AND PAGES 246–47

108 *Articulated bandeau tiara with foliage motif*

Joseph Chaumet (1852–1928)
Circa 1920
Gold, platinum, diamonds
H. 3.5, W. 32 cm
Chaumet Collection, Paris

FACING PAGE Bérénice Bejo wearing a bandeau with foliate patterns in Brady Corbet's 2015 film, *The Childhood of a Leader* (photography by Tom Munro).

In the early 1920s, women's journals such as *Les Modes, La Gazette du bon ton,* and *Vogue* were promoting the silhouette and the art of the parure in the style of the First Empire, in particular reference to Empress Joséphine. The Belle Époque tiara, worn majestically on the top of the head, was gradually being replaced with the bandeau, worn across the forehead at the hairline, on hair that was now cut short. This fashion for wearing hair ornaments low on the forehead à la *Joséphine* fostered the design of bandeaux in a less majestic style than the high crown-like tiaras from the period before 1914, as illustrated by this piece. It is composed of thin foliage scrolls using the "knife-wire" technique, which serves to reduce the thickness of the platinum frame to a minimum, leaving only the stones visible. Thanks to an arrangement of four hinges, this structure molds itself to the shape of the head, making the scrolled foliage motif stand out from the hair, as if by magic. This bandeau was worn by Bérénice Bejo in *The Childhood of a Leader*, a Franco-American film directed by Brady Corbet that won awards at the 2015 Venice Film Festival, loosely based on the short story by Jean-Paul Sartre published in 1939. Note that Bejo wears the bandeau tiara in her hair, not on the forehead, in a manner closer to the Belle Epoque than the Roaring Twenties. R.C./K.H.

109 *Oak leaves bandeau tiara, transformable into a choker*

Joseph Chaumet (1852–1928)
1913
Platinum, diamonds
H. 4, W. 33 cm
Private collection

Produced for the Maison's stock and acquired by Baron Henri Hottinguer, a prominent banker and investor in France in the early twentieth century, on the occasion of his marriage to Miss Marian Munroe, daughter of the New York banker John Munroe, this bandeau has a number of features characteristic of Chaumet's work. With a design of interlinked oak-leaf wreaths, a symbol associated in the West since ancient times with strength, longevity, sovereignty, and divine privilege, mounted on a platinum structure in the form of a series of small diamond-set ovals, this bandeau, each section of which is detachable thanks to a discreet system of hinges, can also be transformed into a choker that molds perfectly to the neck. R.C.

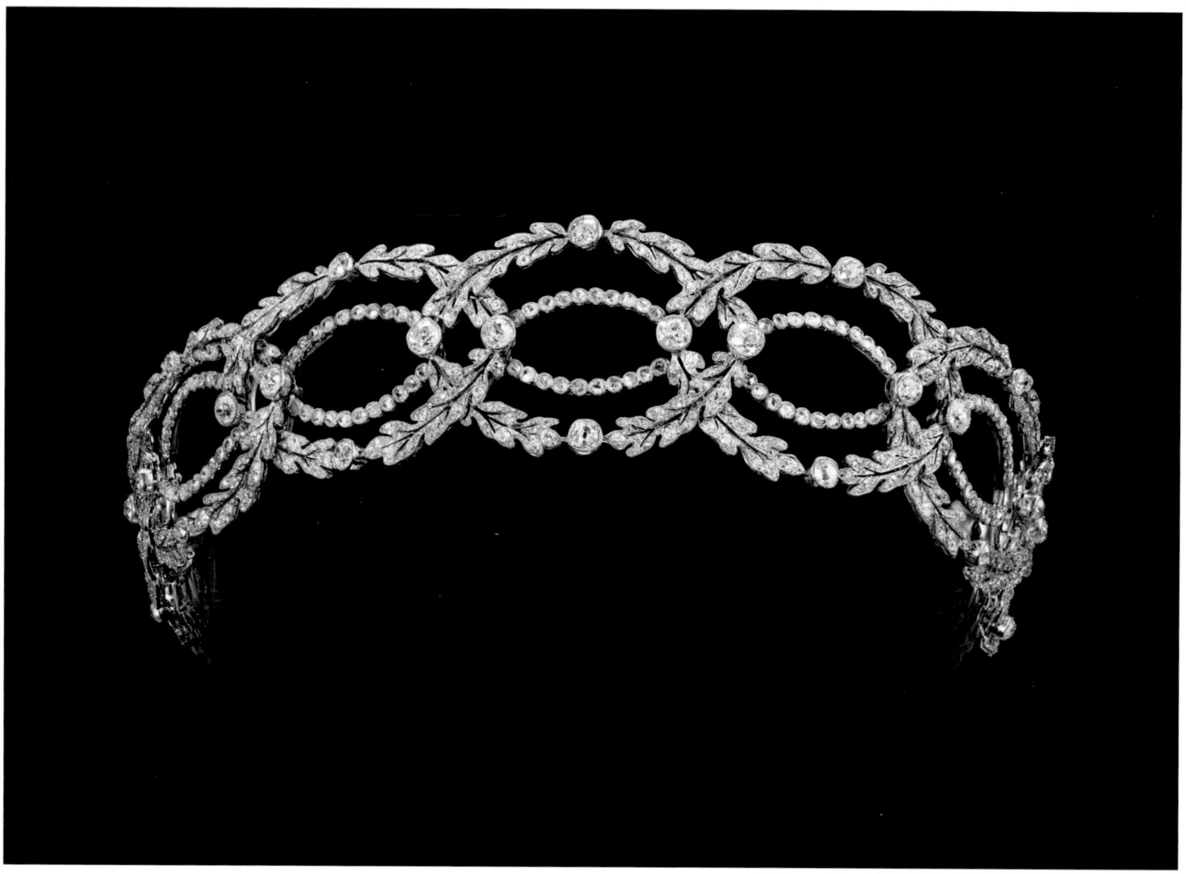

110 *Braid bandeau tiara, transformable into a choker*

Joseph Chaumet (1852–1928)
1921

Platinum, diamonds
H. 4.3, W. 34 cm
Chaumet Collection, Paris

This fully articulated tiara in the art deco spirit features a stylized braid. It can be worn as a bandeau across the forehead, closed to form a crown worn on the top of the head, or transformed into a choker. It thus offered multiple possibilities to its owner, the Marquise de La Roche. This motif proved popular and several versions were produced, with slight variations in the braid design. C. V.

111 *Eight-sapphire bandeau tiara, transformable into a necklace*

Marcel Chaumet (1852–1928)
1921
Platinum, diamonds, sapphires
H. 2.5, W. 39.5 cm
Albion Art Collection, Tokyo

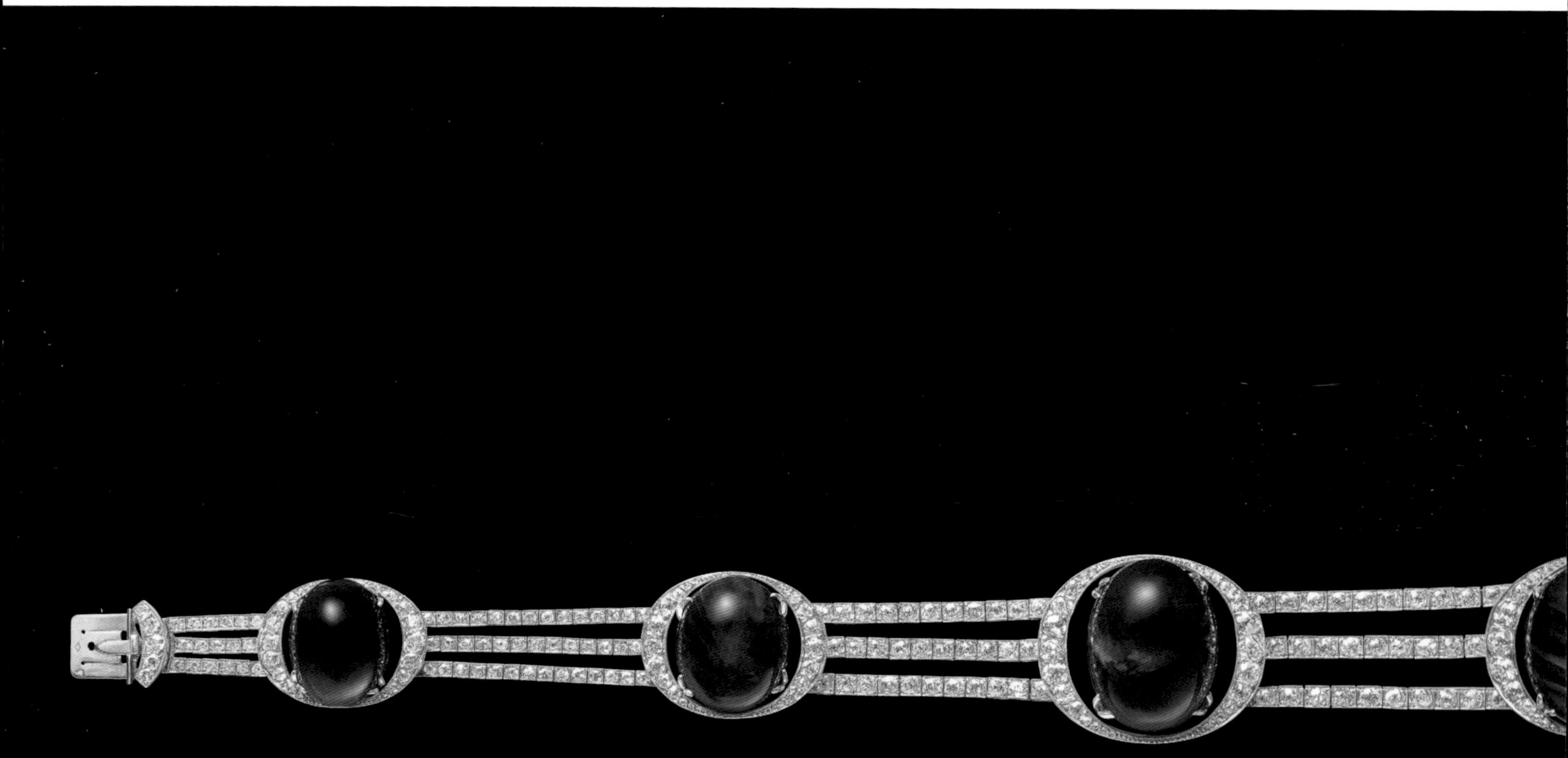

The *garçonne* or flapper look of the 1920s and '30s launched the fashion for short hair, which in turn changed the style of head ornaments. The tiara was replaced by a bandeau, worn low over the forehead near the eyebrows. Designs had clean, geometric, simple lines and often featured strong color contrasts, in combinations of opaque and transparent, faceted and cabochon stones. This head ornament, originally designed as a bandeau of seven sapphire cabochons linked together with three rows of diamonds, was very flexible so that it could be molded to the wearer's forehead. It was later converted into a necklace with the addition of an eighth sapphire. K. H.

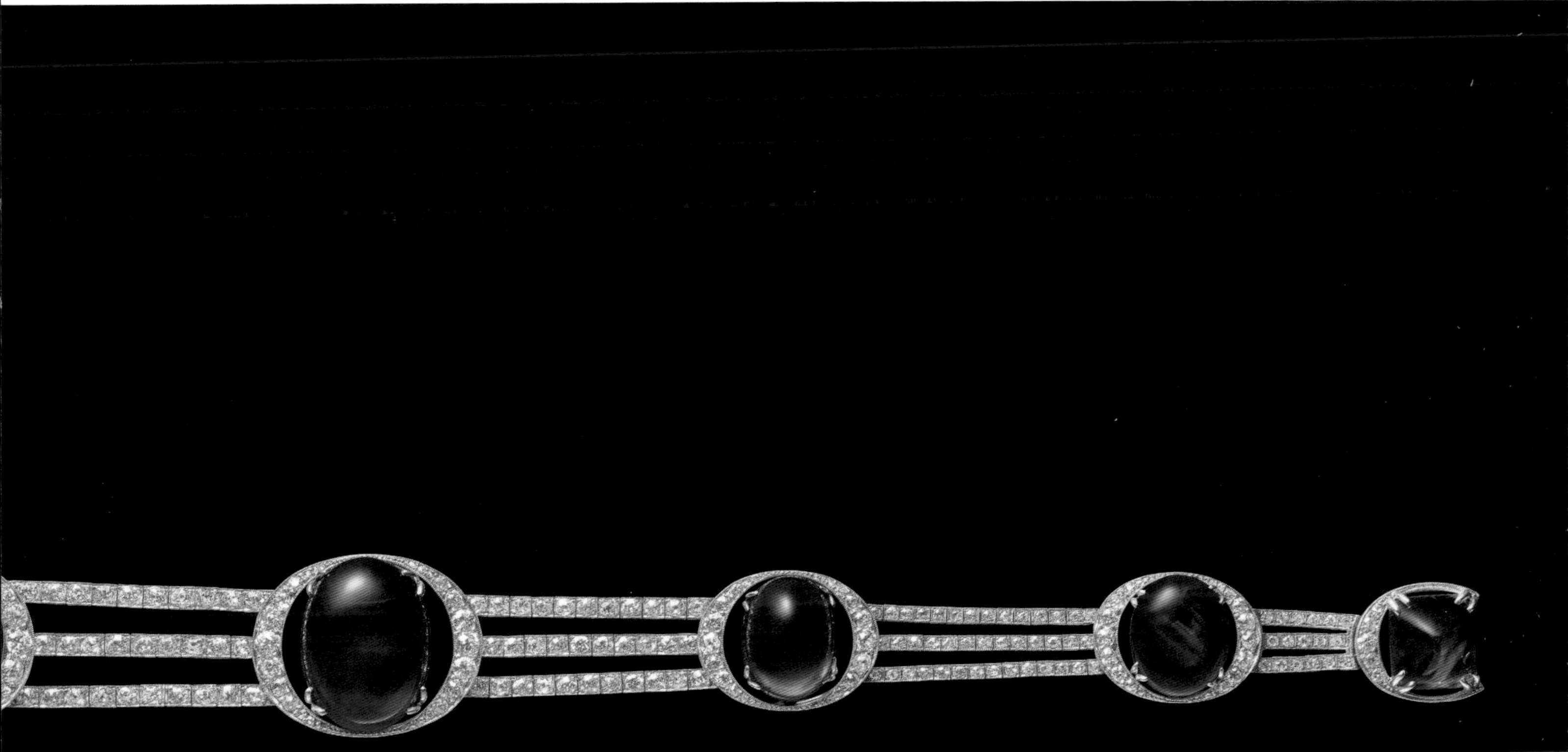

112 *Tiara from the* Bourbon-Parma *parure, transformable into a necklace*

Marcel Chaumet (1886–1964)
1937

Platinum, rubies, diamonds
H. 4, W. 23 cm
The Lin Family Collection, Taipei

In 1935, Chaumet, who had a special relationship with the Spanish royal house, was commissioned to supervise the wedding basket of gifts for Princess María de las Mercedes of Bourbon-Two Sicilies, who was to marry Juan, son of King Alfonso XIII and future count of Barcelona. The pieces produced were such a success that the following year, when Maria's brother Alfonso was to marry Princess Alice of Bourbon-Parma, he asked Chaumet to make three sumptuous parures: the first in pearls and diamonds; the second in sapphires and diamonds; and the third in rubies and diamonds. The prince had inherited jewels from his grandmother, Queen Mária Cristina of Spain, set in old mounts that were no longer fashionable, and so the jewels were deposited with the Chaumet workshops to be unset. Among them was a diamond and ruby parure that had been a gift from Emperor Franz Josef on the occasion of Mária Cristina's marriage to King Alfonso XII of Spain. The stones, of the finest quality, were mounted in a sautoir that could be divided into bracelets, with a pendant that could be worn as a brooch, and also in a bandeau tiara, a pair of earrings, and a different, crescent-shaped brooch. The opulence and quality of the designs of the three art deco-style parures caused a sensation at the time. In 1937, a halo tiara was added to the ruby parure, combining clear-cut art deco forms with a classic elegance. Transformable into a necklace and featuring a row of cushion-cut rubies and a crest of baguette-cut diamonds marking the central peak, it offered a handsome alternative to the bandeau tiara from the same ensemble. C. V.

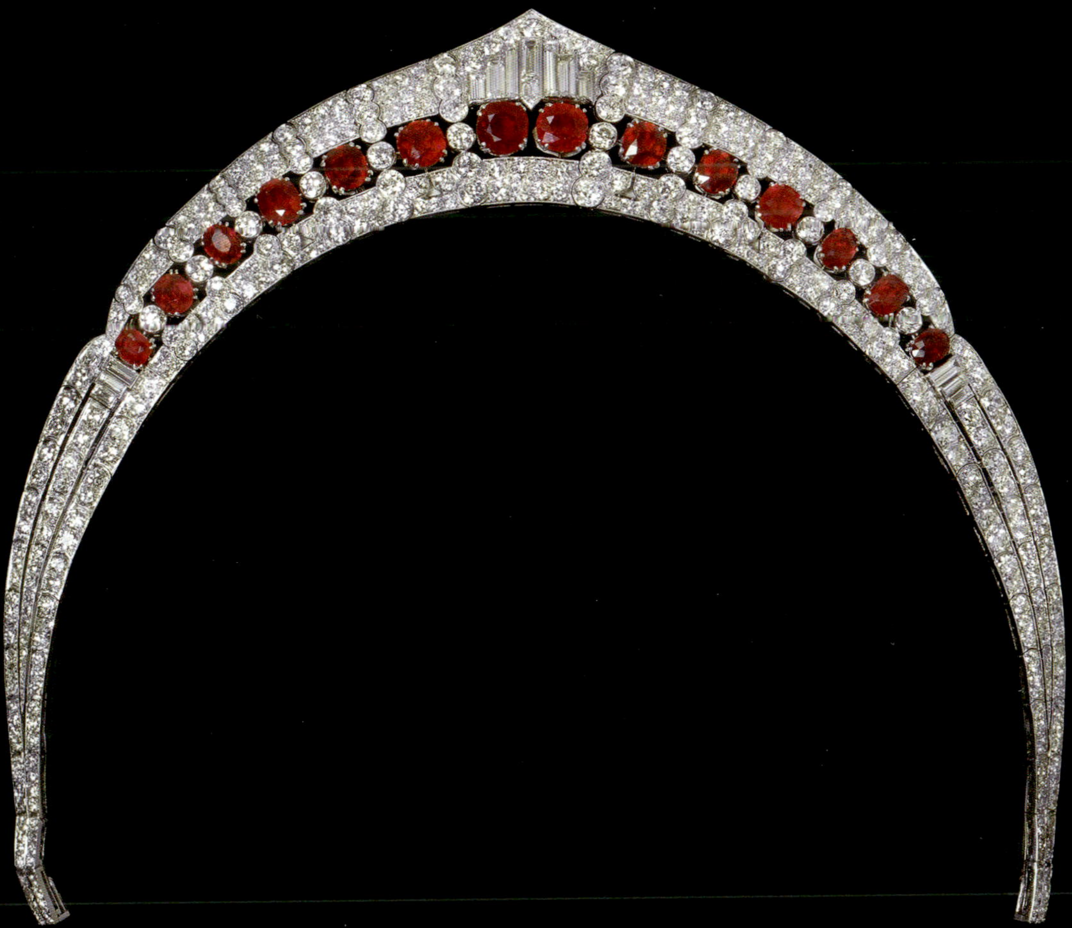

FACING PAGE AND PAGES 256–57

113 *Articulated bandeau tiara*

Joseph Chaumet (1852–1928)
1924

Diamonds, pearls, platinum
H. 2, W. 16.5
Private collection

The articulated bandeau tiara, designed to be molded to the shape of the head, goes back to the First Empire, when jeweled headbands were all the rage as a fashion accessory. "No hat but a bandeau on the forehead," was the recommendation of the *Journal des dames et de la mode* in January 1804. This fashion has endured through the centuries in Chaumet's designs: still the classic head ornament, like a ribbon around the head, it recalls the ancient diadem, from the Greek *diadēma*. K. H.

Articulated bandeau tiara. Print from gelatin silver-bromide glass negative no. 10.053, 1924. Chaumet Archives, Paris.

J. CHAUMET
Sté DE MOREL & Cie
LONDON
NEW BOND STREET
-154-
PARIS
PLACE VENDÔME
-12-

114 *Three hat pins*

Joseph Chaumet (1852–1928)
1912, 1913, and 1914

Gold, platinum, rock crystal, aquamarine, agate, sapphire, diamonds
H. 22.5, W. 3.5. H. 21.5, W. 4. H. 24.5, W. 5.5 cm
Chaumet Collection, Paris

While formal evening attire in the Belle Époque called for the hair to be styled high on the head, glittering with adornments and flattering the face, fashionable daytime outfits would always include a voluminous hat adorned with all sorts of decorative elements, in fabric, feathers, flowers, and so on. These creations were held in place on the head with long pins, often in pairs, which featured ornamental heads, offering multiple creative possibilities to the jeweler. K. H.

115 *Pair of hat pins*

Joseph Chaumet (1852–1928)
Circa 1900
Gold, platinum, enamel, diamonds
H. 27, Diam. 3.1 cm
Chaumet Collection, Paris

116 *Two hat pins*

Joseph Chaumet (1852–1928)
Circa 1915
Platinum, onyx, diamonds
H. 22 , Diam. 2 cm. H. 14, Diam. 3
Chaumet Collection, Paris

FACING PAGE

117 Mary Stuart *aigrette*

Joseph Chaumet (1852–1928)
Circa 1910

Gold, silver, natural pearls, diamonds
H. 10 cm (without the feathers)
Chaumet Collection, Paris

PAGE 262

118 *Meshwork aigrette, transformable into a brooch*

Joseph Chaumet (1852–1928)
Circa 1910

Platinum, diamonds
H. 3.5, W. 6 cm
Chaumet Collection, Paris

As the Belle Époque came to an end, "the party set," as the women's society journal *Femina* described it in 1911, had lost nothing of its taste for festivity and society gatherings. These two jewels that probably date from the same period illustrate the spirit of the times. The aigrette, a head ornament named for the bird's feather adorning it, would be worn at official events for which a tiara was considered too formal. The *Mary Stuart* aigrette, with its plume of feathers, mounted on a V-shaped structure reminiscent of the widow's cap with its central dip worn by the Queen of Scots in the Renaissance, fully exudes this festive spirit. Constructed with very thin, mobile "knife-edge" wires, it projected an exuberant display of diamonds and pearls over the wearer's forehead. Using this same technique, the meshwork aigrette—adaptable as a brooch—also featured a central diamond whose mount was fastened to a meshwork motif. R.C.

PAGE 263

119 *Bunch of grapes brooch, transformable into an aigrette*

Joseph Chaumet (1852–1928)
Circa 1925

Gold, platinum, sapphires, rubies, diamonds
H. 4.5, W. 4.1 cm
Chaumet Collection, Paris

This brooch with a simpler design, but symmetrical and stylized in the art deco style, could be fitted with a plume of feathers to be worn as an aigrette. Its motif is a bunch of grapes, attribute of Bacchus, god of wine and intoxication, and renewal; the "much-cheering Dionysus," as the ancient Greek poet Hesiod described him. Although designed for much less formal events than those requiring a tiara, this aigrette brooch is no less remarkable for the quality of its ten sapphires interspersed with small bezel-set cabochon rubies. R.C.

120 ## Bayadère *necklace*

Joseph Chaumet (1852–1928)
Circa 1920

Platinum, natural seed pearls, sapphire cabochons, diamonds
L. 55.5 cm
Chaumet Collection, Paris

In the early twentieth century, Parisian jewelers established connections with the maharajas, and gained access to their fabulous precious stones, which were recut and remounted in new pieces combining Indian colors and forms with European techniques. Joseph Chaumet sent a mission to India in late 1910 and the Gaekwad of Baroda and the Maharaja of Indore remained important clients of the Maison until the 1930s. These new influences permeated Chaumet's designs, and became an endless source for the refined, stylized motifs of the art deco style.

This Indian-inspired sautoir offers a particularly elaborate example named for the tasseled chains worn by Indian dancers—*bayadère* deriving from the Portuguese *bailhadeira*, meaning dancer. These long necklaces were common among Chaumet's designs in the Roaring Twenties, dazzling adornments that reflected the festive energy of the time. Bayadères lay flexibly against newly liberated bodies, and were made up of multiple strands of tiny natural pearls, sometimes braided and twisted, onto which two pendants could be attached, as here. This design features pearl tassels topped with a platinum ornament studded with sapphires and diamonds, and edged with sapphires. K.H.

121 *Large sautoir of carved stones, transformable into a pair of bracelets*

Joseph Chaumet (1852–1928)
1928–29

Platinum, rubies, emeralds, diamonds, black enamel
L. 103 cm
Louise Hung Collection

The International Exhibition of Modern Decorative and Industrial Arts in Paris in 1925 ushered in the art deco style, in which Joseph Chaumet was one of the great practitioners in jewelry. The *garçonne* or flapper fashion of the 1920s and '30s, which came with women's emancipation, called for new kinds of jewelry with clean lines and simple, geometric forms that suited the modern silhouette adopted by fashionable women—short hair and straight, low-waisted, knee-length dresses. This led to the design of long necklaces, or sautoirs, with geometric motifs.

In this Indian-inspired sautoir, carved rubies and emeralds in the Mogul tradition bring an exotic touch to the piece. The paves of brilliants and baguette-cut diamonds form geometric motifs severely outlined in black enamel. The color contrast formed by the ruby-emerald combination, characteristic of ceremonial Indian jewelry, conjures up the splendor of the East. K. H.

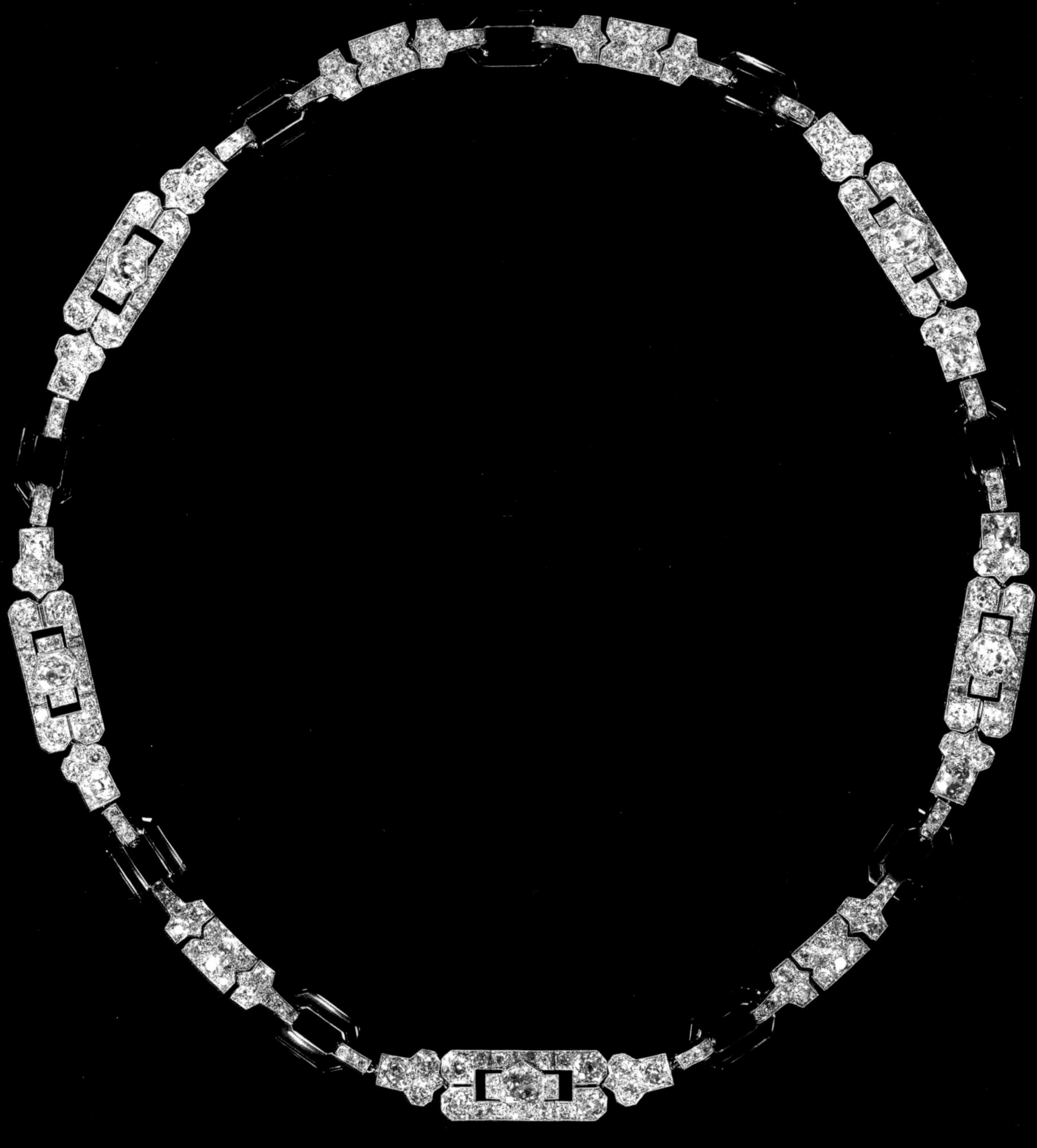

122 *"Chaîne d'huissier" sautoir, transformable into a bracelet*

Marcel Chaumet (1886–1964)
1929
Palladium-plated gold, rock crystal, diamonds
L. 98 cm
Faerber Collection

This sautoir, known as a "chaîne d'huissier" (literally, bailiff's chain), illustrates the fashion for long necklaces throughout the art deco period. Unusual color contrasts were popular, such as emerald and sapphire, or plain monochrome designs like diamonds with onyx. Delicate combinations such as brilliants and polished rock crystal were also sought after. This sautoir features a chain of rock crystal links connected with geometric diamond-set plaques. Often sautoirs could be lengthened as desired, or divided into bracelets. This piece was purchased by Countess Molitor. C.V.

BELOW

123 Valse d'Hiver *brooch*

Chaumet est une Fête collection
Chaumet
2017
Private collection

FACING PAGE

124 Argine la Dame de Trèfle *brooch*

Pierre Sterlé (1905–1978) for Chaumet
Head carved by Robert Lemoine
Circa 1965
Gold, malachite, aquamarine, diamonds
H. 6.5, W. 8 cm
Chaumet Collection, Paris

Avant-garde jeweler Pierre Sterlé designed unique, full-volumed pieces for Chaumet, like this brooch from the mid-1960s "playing cards" series. With the braided hair of gold, head and shoulders carved from an aquamarine, flaring collar of diamonds, and bodice of malachite adorned with gold and diamonds, this brooch illustrates the bold creativity of the 1960s and '70s, marrying gems to hardstones and combining traditional skills with formal exploration. K.H.

125 Aria Passionata *parure: necklace, ring, and earrings*

Chaumet est une Fête collection
Chaumet
2017

Rose gold, ruby, rhodolite garnets, red tourmalines, diamonds
Private collection

"I call the Scala the finest theater in the world, because it provides the most pleasurable experience of music.... It is hard to imagine one larger, more magnificent, more grand, or more new." Few European theaters can boast such praise as that lavished upon the Milanese opera house by Stendhal, who stayed in northern Italy in autumn 1816. Its eighteenth-century interior, lined with red velvet and braid and gilded woodwork, was also the scene of passions, played out in the most famous works of Donizetti, Rossini, Bellini, Verdi, and Puccini, who together wrote the greatest chapter in the history of nineteenth-century vocal music. It was also here, too, that Renata Tebaldi and Maria Callas performed the finest arias of their careers. It was this vibrantly sensual and flamboyant red-and-gold world of the opera that inspired the parure displayed here. With their scarlet stones—pigeon's blood rubies, garnets, and tourmalines—the ring and pair of earrings, together with the necklace, heavy and sumptuous like a stage curtain, with its two brooches that can be worn separately, form a particularly evocative ensemble. R.C.

PAGES 274–75

126 *Scroll tiara*

Joseph Chaumet (1852–1928)
Circa 1907
Platinum, diamonds
H. 4.5, W. 18.5 cm
Private collection

This tiara, whose "knife-wire" structure conceals the metal, thereby bringing out the rows of diamonds, echoes the adornments used in women's attire at the time: flounces, lapels, guimpes, and high collars featuring embroidery and guipure lace. These techniques inspired the Maison's designers, as reflected in the books of designs conserved in the archives. The composition of this tiara, with its perfectly symmetrical row of tall, slender diamond arches along a V-shaped "Mary Stuart" line, indicates that this piece would have been worn high on the hair, requiring a graceful carriage of the head. R.C.

FACING PAGE

127 *Rounded palms tiara*

Joseph Chaumet (1852–1928)
1910
Platinum, diamonds
H. 5.8, W. 15.6 cm
Qatar Museums

According to the society journal *Tatler*, Mrs. Adair lived in a fine house on Curzon Street, London, with "silk-lined walls, some good pictures and any amount of costly French furniture." Many members of London's high society, which included Americans and British aristocrats, commissioned tiaras from Chaumet. Going by the compliments written in the visitors' book, Mrs. Adair appears to have been satisfied with this soft-contoured tiara supplied in 1910. It is geometric in design but has a composition based on the soft forms of the oval, curves, and scrolls, in a fine variation of the modern style. It could be entirely dismantled and worn as a corsage ornament, and the central part could be detached as a brooch. C.V.

BELOW

128 *Scrollwork tiara*

Chaumet
2015
Platinum, diamonds
H. 4.5, W. 14 cm
Collection of Catherine, Hong Kong

FACING PAGE

129 Rhapsodie Transatlantique *necklace*

Chaumet est une Fête collection
Chaumet
2017
Gold, chrysoberyl, tourmaline, tanzanite, diamonds, garnets
Private collection

Performance, as an art form, whether for ceremonies, festive events, or shows, requires a setting, whose form, decor, and function often serve as its metaphor; thus the theater is the best expression of its purpose. New York's Metropolitan Opera, designed by the architect Wallace Kirkman Harrison and opened in 1966, is in itself a symbol of musical performance in its most modern, most elegant, most urban, and most fashionable conception. This monument dedicated to music, decorated with Marc Chagall's huge canvases *The Sources of Music* and *The Triumph of Music* and the avant-garde crystal chandeliers by the Austrian designer Hans Harald Rath, was the inspiration for this aptly colored and sparkling necklace. While the colored stones mounted on diamond-studded leaves recall the painter's poetical compositions, the iridescent aigrette as pendant, on a knife-wire mesh, is reminiscent of the designs by the visionary director of the J. & L. Lobmeyr crystal manufacturer. R.C.

TOP

130 Joséphine *tiara*

Chaumet
2012
Platinum, diamonds
H. 6, W. 16 cm
Chaumet Paris

BOTTOM

131 Joséphine *ring*

Chaumet
2012–18
Gold, diamonds
Private collection

FACING PAGE

132 Joséphine *necklace*

Chaumet
2012
Gold, diamonds
Private collection

The collection created in 2010 and named after Chaumet's first muse, Joséphine, harks back to the tiaras of which the empress was fond. Their elegant design, delicate frames, and superb diamonds and precious stones encapsulate some 240 years of fine craftsmanship. The *Joséphine* collections include every type of jewelry item, also revisiting the Belle Époque aigrette, synonymous with festivity. These tiaras, with the soft, curving lines of their "Mary Stuart" frames, have a magical charm befitting the twenty-first-century woman. K.H.

133 *Scrollwork tiara with pear-shaped rubellites*

Chaumet
2015
Platinum, gold, diamonds, rubellites
Private collection

Heir to the large, foliate tiaras of the Belle Époque, and done in the "grand style" typical of Joseph Chaumet's artistry, this special order reflects the sovereign connotations of a jewel that crowns the head. The imposing tiara is a variation on the theme of scrolling foliage and constantly shifting nature, employing stylized lines and symmetrical patterns to enhance seventeen pear-shaped rubellites. While the original design featured emeralds, the modern version of this tiara is crowned with a variety of tourmaline ranging from deep pink to red, the finest gems coming from Brazil. These pear-shaped rubellites here rise up powerfully to contribute to the sense of elevation. K. H.

Joseph Chaumet (1852–1928), drawing studio, sketch for a scrollwork tiara. Pencil, ink wash, and gouache. Chaumet Collection, Paris.

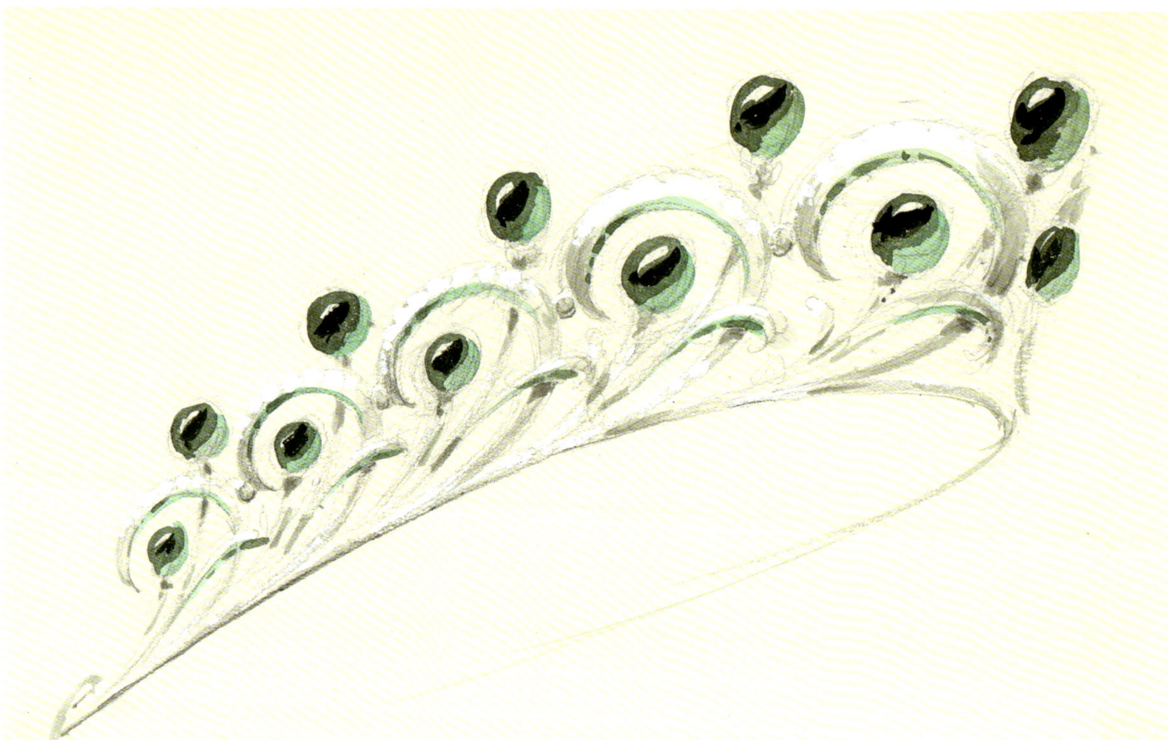

134 Lumières Célestes *parure: Tiara* (pages 286–87)*, sautoir necklace, ring, earrings*

Chaumet
2017
Gold, diamonds, pearls
Private collections

Made for the retrospective *Imperial Splendours: The Art of Jewellery Since the 18th Century* exhibition organized by Chaumet in conjunction with the Palace Museum in Beijing's Forbidden City in 2017, the *Lumières Célestes* parure is a Paris jeweler's glowing tribute to Chinese civilization and its timeless symbols. A meeting of East and West, this set of jewelry evokes the philosophy of Yin and Yang, of the dual nature of opposing yet complementary forces.

The Yin motif of a stylized cloud is a complex esoteric reference, yet also refers to everyday culture in which the Chinese word for "cloud" (yun 云) is related to fortune or luck. Adorning lucky charms and amulets, a cloud—when repeated, as here—suggests endless luck.

Meanwhile, a pearl—the Yang element—symbolizes rebirth and immortality. Pearls from the seas of southern Australia join Akoya pearls from the China and Japan seas to share their subtle iridescence with the glitter of colorless and yellow diamonds whose intense colors display rare homogeneity. Yellow, a fundamental color in Chinese culture, symbolizes wisdom and glory, a glory that the *Lumières Célestes* tiara expresses with beauty and grandeur. Based on a structuring line whose twists evoke the rooftops of imperial palaces and temples, this tiara draws inspiration from the head ornaments worn by performers in the legendary Beijing Opera. Diamonds and pearls levitate thanks to "knife-edge" setting, creating the impression of powerful thrust and majesty, a veritable heavenly halo that illuminates and transcends the woman who wears it. K. H.

SELECT BIBLIOGRAPHY

BABIN, Gustave. *Une pléiade de maîtres joailliers, 1780-1930.* Paris: Imprimerie de Frazier Soye, 1930.

HUREL, Roselyne, and Diana Scarisbrick, eds. *Chaumet Paris: Two Centuries of Fine Jewellery*. Exh. cat. (Paris, Musée Carnavalet, March–June 1998). Paris: Paris Musées, 1998.

LOYRETTE, Henri, ed. *Chaumet: Parisian Jeweler Since 1780.* Paris: Flammarion, 2017.

SCARISBRICK, Diana, ed. *Chaumet: Master Jewellers Since 1780.* Paris: Alain de Gourcuff Éditeur, 1995.

———. *Tiara*. Exh. cat. (Boston, Museum of Fine Arts, March–June 2000). San Francisco: Chronicle Books, 2000.

———. *Timeless Tiaras: Chaumet from 1804 to the Present.* Paris: Assouline, 2002.

———. *Parures du pouvoir—Joyaux des cours européennes.* Exh. cat. (Brussels, Espace Culturel ING, October 2007–February 2008). Brussels: Fonds Mercator, 2007.

———. *Le Grand Frisson, Le Bijou de sentiment de la Renaissance à nos jours.* Paris: Textuel, 2008.

VANDENSANDE, Lesja, ed., et al. *Napoléon et les joyaux de l'empire: Pour l'honneur et pour la gloire*. Brussels: Fonds Mercator, 2010.

PHOTOGRAPHIC CREDITS

t: top; b: bottom

© Chaumet: p. 8, 29, 30, 33, 36, 65–66, 73, 148–49, 154–57, 164, 166, 172–73, 175, 180, 199, 202, 204–5, 206, 212, 218–19, 222, 225, 230–31, 236–37, 240–43, 254, 270, 272–73, 278–87.

Nils Herrmann © Chaumet: p. 2, 4, 25, 39, 53, 55, 56–57, 67–69, 81, 83, 106–7, 110–11, 113, 115–17, 122, 127–29, 131, 134–35, 137–39, 141–43, 151–53, 159–61, 167–71, 182, 184–85, 187, 189–95, 197t, 207, 209–11, 213–15, 220–21, 224, 226–27, 229, 235, 244, 246–48, 250–51, 255–59, 261–63, 265, 271, 274–75.

Bruno Ehrs © Chaumet: p. 20–21, 37, 58–59, 74–75, 96.

p. 12: © Alexis Daflos/The Royal Court SWE; p. 15: © The Walters Art Museum; p. 16: © National Portrait Gallery, London; p. 17: © RMN-Grand Palais (Château de Versailles)/Gérard Blot; p. 19: © Henry Clarke, Musée Galliera/Adagp, Paris 2019/Vogue Paris; p. 22: © RMN-Grand Palais (Musée des Châteaux de Malmaison et de Bois-Préau)/Gérard Blot; p. 26: © RMN-Grand Palais (Château de Versailles)/Gérard Blot; p. 27: © RMN-Grand Palais (Château de Versailles)/Gérard Blot; p. 31: © Ullstein Bild/Roger-Viollet; p. 32: © Yevonde Portrait Archive; p. 35: © Robert Doisneau/GAMMA-RAPHO; p. 44–45: © Courtesy of Albion Art Jewellery Institute; p. 49: © RMN-Grand Palais/Franck Raux; p. 50–51: © RMN-Grand Palais (Musée des Châteaux de Malmaison et de Bois-Préau)/Franck Raux; p. 60–61: © The Museum of Decorative Arts, Prague; p. 62: © Oger - Blanchet; p. 63: © DIVA Antwerp/Dominique Provost; p. 70: © Kunsthistorisches Museum, Vienna/Musée d'Auxerre - Salle d'Eckmühl; p. 76: © Christophe Vachaudez Collection; p. 77: © Cour Grand-Ducale/Vincent Everarts/All Rights Reserved ; p. 78: © Sotheby's; p. 79: © Madame Yevonde/Mary Evans Picture Library; p. 80: © Christophe Vachaudez Collection; p. 82: © DR/Musée Louis-Philippe, Château d'Eu; p. 87: © Musée Masséna, Nice; p. 89: © All Rights Reserved; p. 90: © RMN-Grand Palais (Musée des châteaux de Malmaison et de Bois-Préau)/André Martin; p. 91: © RMN-Grand Palais (Musée des châteaux de Malmaison et de Bois-Préau)/Franck Raux; p. 92–93: © BNP Paribas, Historical Archives/Jacky Prudhomme; p. 95: © RMN-Grand Palais (Château de Versailles)/Gérard Blot; p. 97: © RMN-Grand Palais (Musée des Châteaux de Malmaison et de Bois-Préau)/Mathéus; p. 99: © Manuel Silveira Ramos/Direção-Geral do Património Cultural/Arquivo de Documentação Fotográfica (DGPC/ADF); p. 101: © Geoffroy Moufflet/Archives du Palais de Monaco; p. 102: © RMN-Grand Palais (Musée des Châteaux de Malmaison et de Bois-Préau)/Gérard Blot; p. 103: © RMN-Grand Palais (Musée des Châteaux de Malmaison et de Bois-Préau)/Franck Raux; p. 104: © Sotheby's; p. 108: © Royal Collections, the Netherlands/Arjan Benning; p. 109: © Courtesy of Albion Art Jewellery Institute; p. 112: © RMN-Grand Palais (Domaine de Compiègne)/All rights reserved; p. 118: © RMN-Grand Palais (Domaine de Compiègne)/Franck Raux; p. 121: © Courtesy of Albion Art Jewellery Institute; p. 125: All Rights Reserved; p. 133: © Qatar Museums; p. 136: © Katarina Faerber; p. 147: © Elena Datrino; p. 162: © RMN-Grand Palais/Hervé Lewandowski; p. 165: © Qatar Museums; p. 174: © Régis Grman/Chaumet; p. 179: © Musée de la Vie Romantique/Roger-Viollet; p. 181: © All Rights Reserved; p. 197b: © Qatar Museums; p. 201: © RMN-Grand Palais/Franck Raux; p. 216–17: © Katarina Faerber; p. 223: © Geoffroy Moufflet/Archives du Palais de Monaco; p. 234: © All Rights Reserved; p. 239: © Cyrille Boulay; p. 245: © Bérénice Béjo in the film *The Childhood of a leader*, photography by Tom Munro; p. 249: © Katharina Faerber; p. 253: © Katharina Faerber; p. 267–69: © Katarina Faerber; p. 277: © Qatar Museums.

COVER Sunburst aigrette, Joseph Chaumet (1852–1928), 1916. Gold, platinum, emerald, diamonds. Chaumet Collection, Paris.